Legal Almanac Series No. 2

HOW TO MAKE A WILL HOW TO USE TRUSTS

Based on original Legal Almanac by PARNELL CALLAHAN

This legal Almanac has been revised by the Oceana Editorial Staff

Irving J. Sloan
General Editor

FIFTH EDITION

1986
Oceana Publications, Inc.
Dobbs Ferry, New York

Library of Congress Cataloging-in-Publication Data

Main entry under title:

How to make a will, how to use trusts.

(Legal almanac series ; no. 2)
"This legal Almanac has been revised by the Oceans
Editorial Staff."
Includes index.   87-2999
1. Wills—United States—Popular works.   2. Trusts
and trustees—United States—Popular works.
I. Sloan, Irving J.   II. Oceana Publications, Inc.
III. Series.
KF755.Z9H65   1985   346.7305'4   85-28834
ISBN 0-379-11156-X   347.30654

© Copyright 1986 by Oceana Publications, Inc.

Manufactured in the United States of America

TABLE OF CONTENTS

iii

INTRODUCTION

Through seven reprintings since its original publication in 1948, this Almanac remained unchanged. The rationale lay in the fact that there is very little change in the law as it affects the making and execution of Wills. As a simple introduction of the reading audience to the need for a Will, the mechanics for creating one, and the forms of simpler Wills, the work remained, through the years, completely adequate.

In 1975, however, the original almanac was expanded to adapt to contemporary needs. These are reflected by the fact that the size of estates is no longer a problem reserved to the very wealthy. People now in their middle years have begun to inherit from their parents, adding these assets to their own. Even younger people face the prospect of combined accumulation of their own growing wealth together with accumulated wealth passed on by prior generations. Thus, the matter of a person's Will has become involved with much more than a simple instrument disposing of one's assets. Matters of tax planning have become crucial; and the choice of methods that both save money and expedite the handling of one's estate essential. In this context, the last edition of this Almanac introduced a segment on trusts, inter vivos (while a person is alive) and testamentary (to take effect at death), as well as detailed analysis of the marital deduction - a device for passing property to one's spouse free of estate taxes.

So rapidly do events move, however, the editors concluded that the effect on estates, and therefore, the effect on Wills and Trusts, of the Tax Reform Act of 1976, made it necessary to create a new edition that would include these important considerations. As a result, the current edition becomes in effect a guide to estate and financial planning, in the context of which, Wills and Trusts become instruments of achieving objectives not only in terms of disposition of assets but their tax consequences, as well. On the premise that an informed layman is the key to a lawyer's ability to do the best possible job for his client, this work, in its present form, is conceived.

HOW TO MAKE A WILL HOW TO USE TRUSTS

Chapter I

WILLS IN GENERAL

1. WHAT IS A WILL?

After your death, it is too late to think about the people to whom you wish to leave your property. It is too late then to decide who will own your house, who will drive your car, who will wear your diamond stick pin, and who will get those shares of stock you had nursed so carefully for twenty years. You may have told everyone just what you wanted, but that is no assurance that it will be done. In fact, because you left no will, it is possible that it cannot be done. Now is the time to make your Will.

A Will is the legal declaration of a man's intent to be performed after his death. In early times, a Will applied only to real property while personal property was disposed of by a Testament. Today the distinction has been eliminated, and the instrument, referred to as "Last Will and Testament," disposes of both real and personal property.

2. DO YOU NEED A WILL?

Of course you do. The answer is the same whether you are a millionaire or whether your only property is the shirt on your back.

Suppose you have nothing whatsoever; no money in the bank; no war bonds; no car; no job. You, nevertheless, have some earning potential and some life expectancy. If you should be run down by a truck on the way out of the house tomorrow morning, someone of your relatives would have the right to sue the owner of the truck, and to recover a substantial sum based upon your earning potential, your life expectancy, your pain and suffering, your hospital bill, expenses of your burial and the circumstances of the persons dependent upon you. To whom do you want this sum

1

to go? Unless you have a Will, you may have nothing to say about it. You won't be here and the money will be distributed in accordance with laws of intestacy, which govern when a person dies without a Will, or when his Will is so defective that it cannot be recognized. The laws of intestacy vary from state to state (see Chapter Four), but the distribution is fixed by law. Your wishes do not control.

Suppose John and Mary are a happily married couple with three children. They own a very comfortable house which they bought in John's name. John dies without a Will, believing that a Will is unnecessary since Mary will have the house. After John's death, Mary finds that she cannot carry the house and decides to sell it. However, Mary cannot sell without extended court proceedings. Mary owns only one third of the house, while each child owns two ninths. A special guardian must be appointed and the sale must be approved by the Surrogate's or Orphans' Court. Even then Mary may not touch the money without a court order each time she finds it necessary to make some expenditure.

Helen and Bill have no children, and their house is in Helen's name. But when Helen dies, Bill is not the sole owner. Helen's father, who opposed their marriage, and who has not spoken to Bill for years, comes in for his share of the house and of the stocks which were bought by Bill from his savings, and very carefully placed in Helen's name for her protection.

Tom and Sally separated by mutual consent and went separate ways. Sally went back to work, and accumulated a comfortable nest egg before she died. She had forgotten about Tom, but he nevertheless receives his share of her estate. Her two sisters with whom she lived, receive something, but Tom gets the lion's share.

The Time to make your Will is Now, while you are still alive. Telephone your lawyer today for an appointment.

3. HISTORY OF WILLS

Wills have not been permitted in all stages of history, although we do find them referred to in the Bible. The right to dispose of property by Will did not exist among the early Germans, and in England until comparatively recent times. There were considerable limitations upon the disposition which a man could make of his property, and a man having a wife and children could dispose of only one third of his property by Will. In Roman Law the children were entitled to their share or "legitime" which their father could not defeat by Will. Louisiana, our only civil law state, is the only one which still retains the "legitime," and a man cannot deprive his children of their share of his estate. The "legitime" amounts to one third of his estate if he is survived by one child; to one half if he leaves two children, and to two thirds if he leaves three or more children. The laws of all states except Louisiana are derived from the common law of England, rather than from the civil law of the European Continent. The common law has long since disregarded the limitations on a man's power over his property insofar as his children are concerned. Primogeniture, the custom of giving the oldest son the title to the father's real estate in preference to the other children, was abolished in the United States shortly after the Revolution.

4. PROPERTY NOT SUBJECT TO DISPOSITION BY WILL

Not everything which a man considers "property" may be disposed of by Will, and care should be exercised to take appropriate action to pass title to property or rights which are not included in a man's estate.

a. Insurance policies: Unless an insurance policy is made payable to a man's estate, its proceeds cannot be affected by his Will. A direction in a Will that the policy in the Rock-Bound Life Insurance Company, now payable to son John, is to be paid to wife Mary, will be of no effect. Son John will collect and wife Mary will realize that it pays to consult a lawyer.

b. United States Savings Bonds: Bonds held in the

3

name of one person payable on death to another do not pass under a Will. A provision in a Will directing that such bonds be delivered upon death to a person other than the one named in the bonds will be of no effect.

c. Jointly owned property: Property owned by two persons, as joint tenants, with the right of survivorship will pass by operation of law and cannot be disposed of by Will. This may be because of the nature of the property, or the technical legal title by which it is held, or because the person attempting to make the Will is married, or for some other reason (See Chapter Three). If property is owned by two persons, as joint tenants with the right of survivorship, the survivor becomes the sole owner of the property despite any provisions to the contrary in the Will of the other joint owner.

d. Exempt Property: In most states there is a small exemption set aside for the widow and surviving children which cannot be taken away by Will and which is not included in the estate for tax or accounting purpose.

e. Rights under the Will of a Third Person: A person may will only such property or rights as he possesses at the date of his death. If he dies on January 1st, and on January 2nd, his uncle Beelzebub dies, leaving him a million dollars, the fact that in his Will he disposed of property to be given him by his uncle will be of no effect. He must have had the property or a right to the property at time of his death.

5. WHO MAY MAKE A WILL

The power to make a Will is now regulated by statute in all American jurisdictions. The various restrictions are discussed in this paragraph.

a. Age

(1) Minimum—In most states, the minimum age is twenty-one years. Below this age, a person may not make a Will. However, the age varies from state to state. In some states, a different age is required for the execution of Wills

4

of real and personal property. In all such instances, greater age is required for the disposition of real property. The minimum age requirement in each state is set forth in Chart No. 1.

It should be noted that except in Arizona, Maine, New Hampshire, Texas, Washington and Wisconsin, marriages

CHART No. 1

MINIMUM AGE REQUIREMENT FOR THE EXECUTION OF A WILL

STATE	Minimum Age for Will of Real Property	Minimum Age for Will of Personal Property
Alabama	18	18
Alaska	18	18
Arizona	18 or married	18 or married
Arkansas	18	18
California	18	18
Colorado	18	18
Connecticut	18	18
Delaware	18	18
Dist. of Columbia	Male 18—Female 18	Male 18—Female 18
Florida	18	18
Georgia	14	14
Hawaii	18	18
Idaho	18	18
Illinois	18	18
Indiana	18	18
Iowa	18 or member of armed services	18 or member of armed services
Kansas	18	18
Kentucky	18	18
Louisiana	16	16
Maine	18 or married woman or widow	18 or married woman or widow
Massachusetts	18	18
Michigan	18	18
Maryland	Male 18—Female 18	Male 18—Female 18

5

CHART No. 1 (Continued)
MINIMUM AGE REQUIREMENT FOR THE
EXECUTION OF A WILL

STATE	Minimum Age for Will of Real Property	Minimum Age for Will of Personal Property
Minnesota	18	18
Mississippi	18	18
Missouri	Male 18 —Female 21	Male 18—Female 18
Montana	18	18
Nebraska	18	18
Nevada	18	18
New Hampshire	18 or married	18 or married
New Jersey	18	18
New Mexico	18	18
New York	18	18
North Carolina	18	18
North Dakota	18	18
Ohio	18	18
Oklahoma	18	18
Oregon	18	18
Pennsylvania	18	18
Philippines	18	18
Puerto Rico	14	14
Rhode Island	18	18
South Carolina	18	18
South Dakota	18	18
Tennessee	18	18
Texas	18 or married	18 or married
Utah	18	18
Vermont	18	18
Virginia	18	18
Washington	18	18
West Virginia	18	18
Wisconsin	18	18 or over, or any minor in Military Service
Wyoming	18	18

does not constitute an emancipation, or enable a person below the minimum age to make a Will. In the states named, however, the marriage of an infant, within certain restriction, enancipates him or her to the extent of permitting the execution of a Will, recognizing such a Will as valid. In Maine, a woman under twenty-one, who is either married or a widow, may execute a valid Will, but unmarried men under twenty-one are still held to be lacking in testimentary competence. Washington and Wisconsin also permit any minor in military service, regardless of his or her marital status, to execute a Will. A Will executed by an infant is a nullity and its property passes as if no Will whatsoever had been made. The fact that a person below the minimum ages does not change or revoke his or her Will on attaining the proper age does not validate a Will ˉmade while under age. The capability to execute a Will must exist at the time the Will is made.

(2) **Maximum Age:** There is no age limit beyond which a man may no longer make a Will. A man fifty years of age may be too enfeebled and incompetent to understand the nature of his act, while, on the other hand, Wills made after the testator has passed the century mark have been sustained, and there are innumerable cases on record where Wills made by men and women in their eighties and nineties have been upheld despite strenuous attacks. Where circumstances show that the testator had sufficient control of his or her mental faculties, the Will will be admitted to probate, even as late as thirty years after death, and even where the testator was ninety-eight years old at the time of the execution of the Will. In other cases, where the attending physician has testified that a ninety-six year-old woman was weak and infirm, but had not reached the stage of mental senility before she died, and four months before her death gave unaided instructions to her attorney as to her Will, the Will was sustained. Even where the testator, in his late eighties, was unclean in his personal habits and apparel, suffered lapses of memory, and talked continuously about his military service of fifty years earlier, his Will has

7

been sustained where he understood the nature of his act, the nature and the amount of his property and the disposition which he made it (See Chapter Two on Execution of Wills).

b. Persons of Unsound Mind

It is the soundness of mind at the time the Will is executed which is important. A Will executed by a lunatic who subsequently recovers his sanity, and dies without changing his Will, is invalid, since the testator must have possessed mental capacity at the time the Will was executed. Not every degree of mental unsoundness is sufficient to invalidate a Will. Belief in spiritualism, a lack or disregard of generally accepted moral standards, over-indulgence in alcohol, and even addiction to drugs will not necessarily invalidate a Will, as long as the testator was sane and knew what he was doing at the time he executed the Will. The three acid tests, which must be met before the Will will be recognized, are as follows:

1. Did the testator (person executing the Will) know that he was executing a Will? Did he know that he was doing and what effect it would have?

2. Did he know the nature and extent of the property mentioned in the Will, and of his property in general?

3. Was he aware of the existence of the natural objects of his bounty?

If any doubt exists as to the competency of the testator, or if any doubt may subsequently arise, it is best to prepare extensive affidavits at the time of the execution of the Will, to supply evidence to answer any objections which may be raised. Forms for these affidavits and explicit instructions for their preparation are to be found in Chapter Two.

c. Idiocy

Idiocy, in point of law, is the complete absence of mind or mental ability. Low mentality is no bar to the execution of a Will as long as the person knows what he is doing, and can meet the same tests set forth for persons of sound minds. A moron, with a mental age of 10 to 12 years, or an imbecile with a mental age of three or fours years may, nevertheless, understand that he owns property and may designate the persons to whom he wishes to bequeath or devise property. The fact that a guardian has been appointed for him is no bar as long as he is not insane. As long as he has sufficient mental ability to understand the nature of his Will, he is not precluded from making a testamentary disposition of his property.

d. Aliens

By common law, aliens were not permitted to dispose of their property. Today, however, all states have granted them the right by statute to make Wills of any real or personal property they are entitled to hold while living. The right to make a Will and to dispose of property does not necessarily permit the removal of any property which has been frozen or whose removal has been prohibited by governmental regulations. During the war, property bequeathed or devised by aliens, or by citizens to alien enemies, or to persons in enemy territory, was held by the Aliens Property Custodian until the cessation of hostilities and the removal of restrictions.

e. Convicts

In the absence of statutes prohibiting convicts from making Wills, persons convicted of crime and sentenced to prison, may nevertheless dispose of their property by Will.

f. Married Women

Today statutes in all states permit a married woman to make a valid Will disposing of her property. Under the English Statute of Wills and under the earlier American law, a married woman executing her Will could not dispose of real property at all, and could dispose of personal property only with the consent of her husband. Despite the broadening of the powers accorded to a married woman, however, the present statutes in many states give to the wife, as to the husband, a certain minimum share in the estate of the other, of which the surviving spouse cannot be deprived by the other's Will. Such a share is, however, subject to the debts of the deceased spouse. (See Chapter One, 7a, infra).

6. LIMITATIONS ON THE POWER TO DISPOSE OF PROPERTY BY WILL

a. Disinheritance

Except in the State of Louisiana, the law permits a man to disinherit his children or other near relatives. A child born or adopted subsequent to the execution of the Will will inherit the same share which he would have received had there been no Will, unless the Will specifically provides that it is to remain in full force and effect, notwithstanding the birth of another child or children at any time after the Will is executed. (See Chapter Three, Paragraph 13).

The Right of Election. In most States neither spouse may disinherit the other, and if the testator leaves a will giving to the surviving spouse a lesser amount than that which would have passed to the spouse by operation of law had there been no Will, the aggrieved spouse either may take the property provided by the Will or may exercise a "right of election." The right of election permits the surviving spouse to elect to "take against the Will," and at his or her option, either to accept the provisions of the Will or to take a stated minimum share, usually the share which he or she would have inherited had there been no Will. The surviving spouse must exercise this election within a fixed period of time, varying from 30 days to 2 years. This right of surviving spouse is closely allied to the right of dower, accorded to a surviving wife, and the right of curtesy, accorded to a surviving husband. Chart No. 2 shows whether your State gives the surviving spouse a right of election to take against the Will, and if so, when the right must be exercised.

Even in states where there is a right of election, the prohibition against disinheritance is not absolute. A husband may disinherit a wife who has abandoned him without justification, and at the same time a wife may disinherit a husband who has either abandoned her, or who has refused or failed to support her. Mere cruelty is not sufficient to bar a surviving spouse from right of election; there must be an abandonment, a failure to support, or an actual decree of separation. Even after such a decree, only the guilty party, and not the party in whose favor it was granted is precluded from exercising the right of election. Since the burden of proof will be upon the executors of the deceased spouse to establish to the satisfaction of the probate court that there was such an abandonment or failure to support, the testator who wishes to disinherit his spouse should follow the instruction of Chapter Two relative to the preparation of affidavits at the time of the execution of the will.

CHART No. 2

SPOUSE'S RIGHT OF ELECTION

(H—Husband   W—Wife)

Alabama: Code, 1940, Title 34, §§42, 43; Title 61,   18, 19.
1. H may not take against will of W unless her last will was executed prior to marriage.

2. W may take against will of H. However, if W's separate estate equals or exceeds value of dower, she is not entitled to dower; if it is less, then difference is made up.

3. Period for filing election: Within 6 months after probate of will.

Arkansas: L. 1949, Act 140, §§33, 35.
1. H may not take against will of W unless her last will was executed prior to marriage.

2 W may take against will of H.

11

SPOUSE'S RIGHT OF ELECTION

(H—Husband   W—Wife)

3. Period for filing election: Within 1 month after expiration of time for filing claims.

Colorado: Stats., 1935, c. 176, §37.

1. H may take against will of W if she bequeaths or devises away from him more than 1/2 of her property or estate.

2. W may take against will of H if he bequeaths or devises away from her more than 1/2 of his property or estate.

3. Period for filing election: Within 6 months after probate.

Connecticut: Stats., 1949, §7309, as amended by L. 1949, Pub. Act. 326.

1 H may take against will of W.

2. W may take against will of H.

3. Period for filing election: Within 2 months after expiration of period for exhibiting claims.

Delaware: Code, 1935, §3771.

1 H may take against will of W with respect to real property.

2. W may take against will of H with respect to real property.

District of Columbia: Code, 1940, §18-211..

1 H may take against will of W.

2 W may take against will of H.

3. Period for filing election: Within 6 months after administration granted.

Florida: Stats., 1941, §§731.34, 731.35.

1. H may not take against will of wife.

2. W may take against will H.

3. Period for filing election: Within 9 months after first publication of notice to creditors.

SPOUSE'S RIGHT OF ELECTION

(H—Husband   W—Wife)

Georgia: Code, §31.103.
1. H may not take against will of W.
2. W may take against will of H with respect to real estate.
3. Period for filing election: Within 6 months after probate.

Illinois: Smith-Hurd Stats., c. 3. §§168, 169.
1. H may take against will of W.
2. W may take against will of H.
3. Period for filing election: Within 10 months after probate.

Indiana: Burns Stats., §§6-2332, 6-2333, 6-2334.
1. H may take against will of W.
2. W may take against Will of H.
3. Period for filing election: Within 6 months after probate.

Iowa: Code, 1946, §§633.2, 636.21, 636.22.
1. H may take against will of W.
2. W may take against will H.
3. Period for filing election: Within 2 months after probate or 6 months after notice of probate.

Kansas: Stats., 1935, §§59-603, 59-2233.
1. H may take against will of W.
2. W may take against will of H.
3. Period for filing election: Within 6 months after probate.

Kentucky: Stats., 1942, §§393.020, 392.080.
1. H may take against will of W.
2. W may take against will of H.
3. Period for filing election: Within 12 months after probate.

SPOUSE'S RIGHT OF ELECTION

(H—Husband   W—Wife)

Maine: Stats., 1944, c. 156, §14.
1. H may take against will of W.
2. W may take against will of H.
3. Period for filing election: Within 6 months after probate.

Maryland: Code, 1939, art. 93, §314, as amended by L. 1947, c. 20, and §§16, 317, 318, 336.
1. H may take against will of W.
2. W may take against will of H.
3. Period for filing election: Within 30 days after expiration of notice to creditors.

Massachusetts: Laws, 1932, c. 191, §15.
1. H may take against will of W.
2. W may take against will of H.
3. Period for filing election: Within 6 months after probate.

Michigan: Laws, 1948, §702.69.
1. H may take against will of W.
2. W may take against will of H.
3. Period for filing election: Within 60 days after entry of order allowing or disallowing claims and closing estate to claims.

Minnesota: Stats., 1945, §525. 212.
1. H may take against will of W.
2. W may take against will of H.
3. Period for filing election: Within 6 months after probate.

Mississippi: Code, 1942, §§668, 669, 670.
1. H may take against will of W unless his separate property equals lawful portion in deceased spouse's estate, then no right of election; if value is less than lawful portion, difference is made up.

SPOUSE'S RIGHT OF ELECTION

(H—Husband   W—Wife)

2. W may take against will of H unless her separate property equals lawful portion, then no right of election; if value is less than lawful portion, difference is made up.
3. Period for filing election: Within 6 months after probate of will.

Missouri: Stats., 1939, §333.
1. H may not take against will of W.
2. W may take against will of H with respect to devise of real property.
3. Period for filing election: Within 12 months after probate.

Montana: Stats., 1943, §§5819, 5820.
1. H may not take against will of W.
2. W may take against will of H.
3. Period for filing election: Within 1 year after probate.

Nebraska: Stats., 1943, §§30-107, 30-108.
1. H may take against will of W.
2. W may take against will of H.
3. Period for filing election: Within 1 year after issuance of letters testamentary.

New Hampshire: Laws, 1942, c. 359, §§10-14.
1. H may take against will of W.
2. W may take against will of H.
3. Period for filing election: Within 1 year after death of testator.

New Jersey: (Stats., 1937, §3:39-1.
1. H may take against will of W with respect to real estate.
2. W may take against will of H with respect to real estate.

15

3. Period for filing election: Within 6 months after probate.

New York: Decedent Estate Law, §18.
1. H may take against will of W.
2. W may take against will of H.
3. Period for filing election: Within 6 months after issuance of letters testamentary or letters of administration with will annexed.

North Carolina: (Stats., 1943, §§30-1, 30-2.
1. H may not elect against will of W.
2. W may elect against will of H.
3. Period for filing election: Within 6 months after probate.

Ohio: Throckmorton's Code, §10504-55.
1. H may take against will of H.
2. W may take against will of H.
3. Period for filing election: Within 1 month after service of citation to elect; if no citation, within 9 months after appointment of executor or administrator.

Oregon: Laws, 1940, §17-113; Ore. L. 1949, c. 475.
1. H may take against will of W with respect to personalty.
2. W may take against will of H with respect to realty as well as personalty.
3. Period for filing election: Realty—within 1 year after death of H; personalty—within 90 days after probate.

Pennsylvania: Wills Act, 1947, §§8 (a), 11.
1. H may take against will of W.
2. W may take against will of H.
3. Period for filing election: Within 1 year after probate.

Rhode Island: Laws, 1938, c. 566, §§12, 21.
1. H may take against will of W with respect to real

estate.

2. W may take against will of H with respect to real estate.

3. Period for filing election: Within 6 months after probate.

Tennessee: Williams Code, §§8358, 8359.

1. H may take against will of W.

2. W may take against will of H.

3. Period for filing election: Within 1 year after probate of will.

Utah: Code, 1943, §101-4-4.

1. H may not take against Will of W.

2. W automatically takes will of H where testamentary provision is in lieu of distributive share, unless she elects to take the testamentary provision.

3. Period for filing election: Within 4 months after probate.

Virginia: Code, 1942, §§5121, 5122, 5139-b.

1. H may take against will of W.

2. W may take against will of H.

3. Period for filing election: Within 1 year after probate.

Vermont: Laws, 1933, §§2955, 2965.

1. H may take against will of W.

2. W may take against will of H.

3. Period for filing election: Within 8 months after probate.

West Virginia: Code, 1943, §§4091, 4130.

1. H may take against will of W.

2. W may take against will of H.

3. Period for filing election: Within 1 year after probate.

Wisconsin: Stats., 1947. §§233. 13, 233, 14, 233, 23.

1. H may not take against will of W.

2. W may take against will of H.

3. Period for filing election: Within 1 year after probate.

The right of election is a personal right, and dies with the surviving spouse. If not exercised in the lifetime of the surviving spouse, it is lost forever. It may be waived, either before the death of the testator, by a specific waiver in writing, or after the death of the testator, by failing to exercise the right, or by executing a written waiver. Therefore, if your mother or your aunt has such a right, your lawyer, immediately upon learning or suspecting that the Will does not provide her with the legal minimum, will prepare a written form of election to renounce the provision of the Will, and will have her execute it immediately. He will not sit back and wait for developments, since such a course may leave you, as her executor, with no choice but to accept the provisions of the will which wholly or partially disinherit her.

Community Property. The law of community property is in effect in eight jurisdictions. Under this provision of law, property acquired by the husband and wife, or by either of them, during coverture, (the legal state of a married woman) otherwise than in certain specified ways, is community property. This creates a form of partnership between husband and wife, in regard to property acquired by either spouse after marriage. It does not apply to property which belonged to either spouse at the time of the marriage, or to property acquired after marriage through gift, devise, descent or in exchange for other separate property. The doctrine of community property was unknown at common law, and is of continental origin, having existed in the Teutonic, French and Spanish systems of law. It is in effect, in varying degrees, in the following states:

Arizona, California, Idaho, Louisiana, Nevada, New Mexico, Texas and Washington.

The disposition of community property varies somewhat in the community states. In Arizona, California, Idaho and Louisiana, upon the death of either spouse, one half of the community property belongs to the survivor. In Nevada and New Mexico, upon the husband's death, one half of the community property is owned by the wife, while on the wife's death, the entire community property vests in the husband. In Texas the surviving spouse takes title to the entire community property, if there are no surviving children, and to one half if the deceased spouse is survived by any children or other descendants. In Washington, the surviving spouse takes title to one half of the community property while the remaining one half is divided between the children and the surviving spouse.

Divorce. An absolute or final decree of divorce terminates the right of election (Chapter I, 6a, Chart 2), and neither husband nor wife has any right to any part of the estate of a divorced spouse. This applies equally to both the "innocent" and the "guilty" party, and applies whether the divorce was granted on grounds of extreme physical cruelty, or adultery, or because of two years living separate and apart. A separation or limited divorce does not affect the right of election of the injured or successful party, but an absolute divorce wipes out the rights of the injured or innocent party as well as those of the guilty party.

b. Charities

Almost all state statutes regulate to some degree the amount and the nature of bequests or devises to charity. Generally, a testator or testatrix leaving a surviving spouse, child, descendant or parent may not will more than half his estate to charity, or for scientific, literary, religious, benevolent or missionary purposes. On the other hand, relatives other than those named have no right to contest such a devise or bequest. Such gifts are not against public policy, and will be sustained unless they violate the statutory restrictions of the particular state in which the testator is domiciled at the time of his death. Your lawyer will give you the particulars of the restrictions in force in your state, and will tell you who may object to a bequest or devise to a charity, as well as the maximum amount which may be given to a charity rather than to a relative.

If you have one or more favorite charities, and would

like to remember them in your Will, give all the details to your lawyer. The charity may be incorporated under a name altogether different than the name under which it is known to you, and its purposes may be limited under the laws of your state. Let your lawyer make an inquiry to ascertain whether the gift, and the purpose which you have in mind, may be made and accepted legally, and may be adequate for the purpose for which you have earmarked it. If it is not, do you still want the charity to have the benefits, to use as it sees fit? Be sure to tell your lawyer all about it.

c. Public Policy

One is not permitted to do, after death, anything which the law will not sanction during life. Consequently, a provision in a Will which is contrary to public policy, or injurious to the public good, will not be permitted. A bequest of a named beneficiary, on condition that he or she remain unmarried, is contrary to public policy, and the limitation is of no effect. However, a prohibition against remarrying, or against marrying a specific person, or outside a specified religious faith is not contrary to public policy, and does not fall within the prohibition. A bequest to the Communist Party would be another example of one which would not be upheld; likewise an attempted bequest to a government or organization attempting to overthrow a government with which the United States maintained diplomatic relations has been held invalid.

20

Chapter II

THE EXECUTION AND REVOCATION, AND PRESERVATION OF YOUR WILL

1. GENERAL INSTRUCTIONS

Your Will must be subscribed or signed by you at the end of the Will, in the presence of all of your witnesses, who must then sign their names as witnesses. In all states, there must be at least two witnesses, while some states require three. You must follow your attorney's instructions in detail, since a faulty execution, and a failure to comply with all the formalities which the law prescribes, may invalidate your Will, and leave your intentions unfulfilled to the same extent as if you had died without a Will. In fact litigation costs may eat up all or the major part of your estate.

2. WITNESSES

It is best to have one witness in excess of the number required by law. Chart No. 3 tells you just how many witnesses are required by the laws of your own state. If your state requires only two witnesses, it is best to have three. and if your Will is to be executed in a state which requires three witnesses, you should have four witnesses. You will want this extra witness not only because it will make your Will easier to probate, but because you may die a resident of a state which requires only two witnesses, but at the same time own property in a state requiring three witnesses.

Your witnesses should be people who know you, and, if possible, persons who are younger than you, since, in the normal course of events, there is a probability that they will outlive you. The longer they have known you, the better. Relatives do not necessarily make the witnesses. Do not permit anyone whom you name in the Will to be a witness.

21

Your executor, and the attorney who draws your Will, should be witnesses wherever possible.

If you should make the mistake of using as a witness a person named in the Will as beneficiary, the Will is not invalidated, but if it cannot be proved or admitted to probate without the testimony of the beneficiary, the devise or legacy to the beneficiary is void, the balance of the Will being permitted to stand. If the beneficiary is a person who would have received a share of your estate if you had died without a Will, he will receive either the share which you left him under the Will, or the share which he would have inherited if you had died without a Will, whichever is smaller. If there are only two witnesses, and one of them is named as a beneficiary, the devise or bequest to him may be void.

When you decide to make your will, call your lawyer and make an appointment to see him. Make a list in which you give him the full names and birthdays of your wife and children, as well as your parents and your brothers and sisters. State the details of all your property, and prepare a brief outline of what you want to do with it—in other words, state your wishes, or your Will. If your Will is to be a simple one, your lawyer can probably dictate it to his secretary while you wait, and you can execute it immediately. If your lawyer tells you that you will probably be able to execute your Will in one visit, ask him whom you should use as a witness.

Chart No. 3

NUMBER OF WITNESSES REQUIRED FOR VALID EXECUTION OF A WILL

I. The following States Require Three Witnesses:

Connecticut	New Hampshire
Georgia	Philippine Islands
Louisiana	Puerto Rico
Maine	South Carolina
Massachusetts	Vermont

II. The following States Require Two Witnesses:

Alabama	Montana
Alaska	Nevada
Arizona	New Jersey
Arkansas	New Mexico
California	New York
Colorado	North Carolina
Delaware	North Dakota
District of Columbia	Ohio
Florida	Oklahoma
Hawaii	Oregon
Idaho	Pennsylvania
Illinois	Rhode Island
Indiana	South Dakota
Iowa	Tennessee
Kansas	Texas
Kentucky	Utah
Maryland	Virginia
Michigan	Washington
Minnesota	West Virginia
Mississippi	Wisconsin
Missouri	Wyoming

3. THE PAPERS COMPRISING YOUR WILL

After your lawyer has prepared your Will, he will hand it to you to read before you sign it. He will probably discuss it with you paragraph by paragraph, and clause by clause. If there are any corrections, or changes, it will be necessary for the Will to be retyped. He may have left the date blank, not knowing just when you would call at his office to sign your Will. In that case the date should be written or type-written in before you actually sign the Will. Your lawyer will not fasten the pages of the Will together until you have read it for possible errors or corrections. Afte you have approved it, if it is more than one page, he will fasten the pages together with a cover in such a way that it will be impossible for you or anyone else to remove or substitute a page without actually destroying the entire Will. This is usually accomplished by the use of a stapling machine, or by using hot sealing wax and ribbons, through the pages and the cover. Any change, correction or alteration must be called to your lawyer's attention before the pages are fastened together, or if the entire Will is contained on one page, before the page is fastened to the cover. Your lawyer will tell you that any erasure, correction, striking out or insertion will be presumed to have been made after the execution of the Will, and not in the presence of witnesses.

4. ACTUAL EXECUTION OF THE WILL

After your first conference, your lawyer will decide on the witnesses. He may decide to be a witness himself, and to have his partner or assistant, or his secretary serve as a witness. You may be certain that he will prefer, and if at all possible, will select witnesses who

1. Are younger than you (the chances are that they will outlive you.);
2. Are in good health (their chances of outliving you are increased);
3. Have known you for some period of time (they know that you are competent);
4. Live somewhere near your home (they are easy to reach when they are needed);
5. Are not named in the will as legatees or devisees (See the preceding section).

Your lawyer will call you and the witnesses into his office, and will arrange to have everyone seated around a desk or table. He will then ask, "Mr. Client, is this your Last Will and Testament?

"Have your read it?"

"Do you wish to make any additions, corrections or changes?"

"Are you satisfied that this Last Will and Testament as it now drawn, expresses your Will?

"Are you now prepared to execute this Will?"

After you have answered "Yes" to all these questions,

he will place the Will on the desk before you. You will then take your pen, and will say to the witnesses:

"This is my Last Will and Testament, which I am about to execute. I ask each of you to witness my signature and my execution of the Will."

You will then initial each page (except the last page) if the Will is more than one page long, and will sign your name at the end of the Will. After you have signed the Will, you will hand it to the first witness, who will then sign his name and address as a witness. You and the witnesses will remain seated around the desk throughout the ceremony or ritual of execution. The second and third witnesses, and if necessary, the fourth witness, will then sign their names and addresses, and your Will will be complete.

Under no circumstances should you ever execute your will in duplicate. If you sign more than one copy, all copies signed by you must be produced before the Will can be admitted to probate, and if one or more copies are lost, there will be a presumption that the Will was revoked.

As soon as your Will is complete, your lawyer will take the carbon copies which were prepared when the original Will was typewritten and will confirm them by typewwriting your name and the names and addresses of the witnesses on the copies. He will then prepare an affidavit for each of the witnesses, and one to be sworn to by him. He will do this because you all hope that it will be a long time before the Will is presented for probate. You yourself certainly hope that it will be at least twenty years, and do you remember where you were twenty years ago today? You may move to another part of town, or your business may keep you so occupied that you will drift away from the close friend who was kind enough to accompany you to your lawyer's office to serve as witness. Twenty years from now he may have forgotten completely the day he accompanied you to your lawyer's office, but his affidavit will serve to refresh his memory, and to remind him of the details which will be so necessary a few years hence. His affidavit will be substantially as follows:

State of New York) (Name of your State)
)
County of New York) (Name of the county in which your
                   lawyer's office is located)

John Goodfriend, being duly sworn, deposes and says:

1. I have known William Testator for seven years. I
first met him (Here state the details of acquaintance, its
extent, and any other pertinent details showing how often
the witness has seen the testator)

2. State what the witness knows of the Testator's intelligence, competency and general occupation, such as (at
this point Mr. Testator is a Supervisor in charge of a sales
crew of twelve persons. His work consists of —————.)

3. State details of how witness happened to be selected to witness the Will, such as
On Monday, January 20th, 1947 Mr. Testator met me
outside the office at a quarter to nine in the morning, and
asked me whether I would have lunch with him today,
Friday, January 24th, and whether I could accompany him
to his lawyer's office to witness his will.

4. State details of execution of Will, such as:

Mr. Testator read through the two pages holding the
first page in his hand as he read the second. Mr. Volume
then said to him, "Is this your last Will and Testament?"
and Mr. Testator said "Yes, it is." Mr. Volume then asked
him whether he had read it and whether he wanted to
make any additions, corrections or changes. Mr. Testator
said that he had read the Will and that is was perfectly
satisfactory to him. Mr. Volume then asked him "Is this
your own Will which you are now about to execute?"
Mr. Volume then handed Mr. Testator a card and said to
him "Will you now request each of us to be your witnesses?"
Mr. Testator held the card in his hand for a minute and then
put it down on Mr. Volume's desk and said "This is my Last
Will and Testament which I am about to execute. I ask

each of you to witness my signature and my execution of the Will." He then initialed the first page of his Will and signed his name on the second page. Mr. Volume then reached across the desk and took the Will, blotted Mr. Testator's signature and signed his own name and address beneath Mr. Testator's. He then handed the Will to Mr. Young who also signed his name and address. Mr. Young stood up and handed the Will across the desk to me, then sat down while I signed my name and address. Mr. Testator then pressed a button again and the young lady came back into the room. Mr. Testator then dictated this affidavit and asked the young lady to prepare it as quickly as possible. He said that he would prepare his own affidavit, and that of Mr. Young after Mr. Testator and I had left.

Sworn to before me this
24th day of January, 1947.   John Goodfriend
                                                            (signed)

Arthur Young
Notary Public for the State of
New York, residing in New York County
County Clerk's No. Y932
Commission expires March 30, 1948

After you and your witness have left the office or, if you are not in too great a hurry, while you are there your lawyer will prepare the affidavits of the other witnesses. He may prepare only one affidavit for himself, if the third witness, such as our Mr. Young, is another attorney in his office. In that case, the third witness will sign his name along the margin or at the foot of the affidavit of the attorney but if there is any possbility of his not being available, the lawyer will usually prepare separate affidavits. Lawyers as a rule are excellent witnesses since they tend to remain in one place for a long time. It is not uncommon to find a lawyer in the same office twenty years later and as a rule he can be found by a quick reference to the telephone book. A doctor will also be a good witness since he must renew his license annually, and can be located through the State

Department of Education. Try to avoid using engineers whose work may send them from one state to another and other persons whose occupations are not conducive to their remaining in one spot.

Mr. Volume's affidavit will be substantially as follows:

State of New York)
) ss:
County of New York)

Thomas Volume being duly sworn, deposes and says:

1. I am an attorney and counselor at law duly admitted to practice in the State of New York. I maintain my office at 37 Wall Street in New York City.

2. (Here the lawyer will state how long he has known the testator and how he happened to draw the will.)

3. (Here the lawyer will set forth his conversations with the Testator in connection with the drawing of the Will) such as, "On January   ,"

4. In this paragraph the lawyer will state the details of the execution, either independently, or referring to the affidavit of the witness, such as .... The Will was then executed by Mr. Testator, and in his presence I dictated Mr. Goodfriend's Affidavit, telling Mr. Goodfriend to make any corrections which he saw fit.

5. Mr. Testator has always impressed me as a capable and alert business man and has always been congenial and likeable. He is of superior intelligence and in the preparation of his Will, we discussed the provisions to be made for his wife and three children.

Sworn to before me this
24th day of January, 1947   **Thomas Volume**
Arthur Young
Notary Public for the State of New York
residing in New York County
County Clerk's No. Y932
Commission expires March 30, 1948

I have read the above affidavit and concur in the statement relative to the execution of the Will and my acquaintance with Mr. Testator. I have always considered Mr. Testator as a capable and likeable person and it was a pleasure to do business with him.   Arthur Young

If you intend to disinherit your wife, your husband, any of your children or your brothers and sisters, if you have no wife or children, your attorney's affidavit will go into considerably more detail to show your knowledge of their existence and the fact that you have not forgotten them. He will have you state to him and will incorporate for his own affidavit, and in the affidavits of the other witnesses, your reasons for such disinheritance. He will also go into more detail as to your competence and your testamentary capacity.

5. PRESERVATION OF YOUR WILL

After you have died, someone will have the task of probating your Will and carrying out its provisions. In order to facilitate his work, the original Will should be kept with the original affidavits together with a list of all of your property. This list should include your real estate, bank accounts, stocks, bonds, safe deposit vaults and even your insurance policies. Your insurance policies, unless they are made payable to your estate, do not pass under the Will but they will nevertheless require certain formalities before their proceeds can be paid to your beneficiaries.   Get several copies of your birth certificate and leave them with the Will.   Your lawyer will prepare one large envelope in which he will place (1) your original Will, (2) the original affidavits, (3) your list of property and (4) your birth certificate. He will give you this envelope to take with you and tell you to keep it in your safe or safe deposit vault. If you do not have a safe or a safe deposit vault, buy a metal strong box to preserve the Will, in the event of fire. Your lawyer will keep a copy of the Will and a duplicate original of the affidavits. He will also give you a copy of the Will and copies of the affidavits. The copies should be kept separate from the original. If the original Will is lost or destroyed by accident or casualty, it may still be proved and its provisions carried out. If this happens, the affidavits will be of inestimable value.

6. REVOCATION OF YOUR WILL

A. General

One of the advantages of a Will over a deed or contract is that is can be revoked at your pleasure. A Will does not become permanent until your death. If you enter into a contract you may be subject to a lawsuit if you attempt to change your mind. If you execute a deed, you may not be able to change your mind at all. A Will, however, may be changed so often as you, yourself, change your mind. Even a statement in a Will that it is final does not render it irrevocable, or prevent its change. Even a Will which is "irrevocable" by virtue of a contract may be revoked, and the subsequent Will admitted to probate.

Keep your Will in a safe place. Where your Will was last seen in your possession, and cannot be found after your death, there is a presumption that you, yourself, have destroyed the Will and have thereby revoked it. Even if you showed the Will to someone shortly before your death, if it cannot be found, you will be presumed to have revoked it by destroying or otherwise disposing of it.

You are cautioned in Paragraph 4 of this Chapter, not to execute your Will in duplicate. If, however, you disregard this warning, and did in fact execute two copies of your Will, it will be necessary for your executor to produce both executed copies if the Will is to be admitted to probate. If only one copy can be found, the presumption of revocation by destruction will prevail.

Your lawyer will point out to you, however, that this presumption of revocation by destruction does not arise where someone else was the custodian of your Will. If the custodian is unable to produce your Will, its contents and execution may be subject to proof as a lost Will.

B. Express Revocation by Written Instrument

The best way to revoke your Will is to make a subsequent Will which includes an express clause of revocation, as outlined in Paragraph 4 of Chapter 3. If you fail to include this express revocation of prior Wills, your new Will will revoke the old one only in so far as they are inconsistent. Even then, the court will do all it can to reconcile the inconsistent provisions, and your two Wills may add up to something which, while admitted to probate, and construed by the court, will not be what you want and will not in fact be your Will.

Suppose, however, you do not want to make a new Will, you merely want to revoke and recall the old one, and being meticulous, you want to execute some written instrument of revocation. Tell your lawyer about it. The revocation of your Will is just as techincal and beset with pitfalls as the execution of your original Will. The same formalities must be observed. Even a declaration sworn to by you before a notary public, acknowledging your desire to revoke your Will, is insufficient. Unless the revocation is executed in precisely the same manner as your Will, it will be of no effect. As a matter of fact, in 1918 Margaret McGill, a resident of New York, wrote to her doctor asking him to destroy a Will which she made in favor of one of her friends. The letter was signed by two witnesses but since it merely contained instructions to revoke the Will, and was not in itself a revocation, the Will was admitted to probate.

C. Destruction or Mutilation

If you destroy, burn, or mutilate your Will, while you yourself have possession of it, the Will will be revoked provided that in the accomplishment of such destruction or mutilation you actually intended to revoke the Will. While this manner of revocation has the advantage of greater

31

secrecy, it nevertheless is subject to the disadvantage that the presumption of revocation may be overcome. If you, yourself, burn, tear, cancel or destroy the Will with such intent, that is sufficient. If, however, you request someone else to destroy the Will, the destruction must be made in your presence and must be proved by at least two witnesses. We have seen how Miss McGill's letter of instruction was insufficient. She did not comply with the strict requirements of the law and her Will remained in full force and effect.

Where you have personal possession of your Will, and, while leaving it with your papers, you tear it to pieces, cut off your signature, or otherwise mutilate it in such a way as to show a revocation, the revocation will be effective only if the Will in its mutilated or destroyed state is found among your papers. Where it is found torn, cut, mutilated or marked among the papers of another person, there is no presumption of revocation, and the Will will be given effect according to its original tenor.

D. Changes and Alterations

In Paragraph 4 of this Chapter, you are shown what your lawyer will do about making corrections prior to the execution of your Will. You saw that he would not permit a crossing out or changing but would require the entire page or, if necessary, the entire Will to be retyped.. He did this because any mutilation, cancellation or alteration of the provisions of the Will are presumed to have been made after the execution of the Will. You cannot change your Will after it has been executed unless you comply with the same formalities necessary for its execution. The change must be executed by you in the presence of the proper number of witnesses (two or three, depending upon your State) and must set forth just what you want to do. Mr. Donity, a resident of New York, attempted to change his Will by having his attorney's stenographer remove and rewrite three pages sometime after his Will was executed. He never re-executed the Will and the stenographer never told the lawyer just what had happened. After Mr. Donity's death, his Will was admitted to probate but not in its changed form. The original Will, with no alterations, was given effect.

Many lawyers follow the sound practice of fastening to the Will with a paper clip, a small sheet of paper with the word "Warning" printed in large red letters, over the instruction:

> "This is an original Will. Any alteration or erasures may void the Will. Do not attempt to change the Will without consulting a lawyer.
>
> Thomas Volume
> Attorney-At-Law
> Elmira, New York."

E. Revocation by Operation of Law

(1) Marriage.

Except in states where disinheritance is permitted (see Chart No. 2) your marriage after the execution of your Will revokes your Will to the extent of permitting your wife or husband to receive from your estate, the share which he or she would have received if you had died without a Will. If you want your Will to remain in effect, despite your marriage, it will be necessary for you to make adequate provision for your wife or husband or to have him or her execute a waiver of the right of election (see Chapter One, Paragraph 6a).

(2) Birth of children after the execution of your Will.

While all states, except Louisiana, permit you to disinherit your children, most of them require you to make some mention of them, to show that you had them in mind at the time you executed your Will. The general rule is that a child born after the execution of the Will, and not provided for in the Will, may take part of your estate in spite of the Will. His birth does not specifically revoke the will but merely nullifies it in so far as it applies to the inheritance or part of the estate to which the child would have been entitled if there had been no Will. The fact that you had other children born before you made your Will and that you made no provision for them, does not, in most jurisdictions, have any effect. Your after-born child may still claim his inheritance.

You can, however, provide that your Will remain in full force and effect by including a clause to the effect that it is to remain in effect notwithstanding the birth of children subsequent to its execution. For such a clause see Paragraph 13 of Chapter 3.

(3) Ademption.

Where property is the subject of a specific legacy or devise and subsequent to the Will, the property is disposed of or its nature is so changed that it is incapable of delivery in the form provided for in your Will, it is said to be "adeemed," and the legacy becomes extinct to the same effect as if you had actually revoked it. The change of the property, itself, and not your intention at the time of the change, or at the time you originally executed your Will, is the controlling factor in accomplishing ademption. It occurs whether the change, loss or disposal of the property is the result of your conscious act, or whether it is the result of some factor over which you have no control.

If you own certain property or stock and feel that you may dispose of it or may take advantage of a good offer of sale but nevertheless want your legatee to benefit, it is best to include in your Will a clause to the effect that the proceeds of the property, if sold during your lifetime, be bequeathed to your legatees. If you do not make such a provision, your devise or bequest will fail upon the change of the nature of the property. A mere disposition or insubstantial change in the nature of the property will not result in an ademption. Where Mrs. Campbell bequeathed "my diamond brooch" and subsequent to the execution of her Will, sold the brooch and bought a new one in its place, the new brooch was held to pass under the Will. A legatee of Mrs. Martin, who had bequeathed 40 shares of $100, par value stock, was permitted to receive, on Mrs.

Martin's death, 160 share of $25 par value stock received during Mrs. Martin's life time, in exchange for her original stock.

7. HOLOGRAPHIC WILLS

A holographic Will is one entirely in the handwriting of the testator. It requires no witness: it need not even bear a date. It does not need testamentary language, and a letter written and signed by Gus Lavant, a trapper in Alaska—"After death please send all to the Red Cross; they might be able to do good with the little I leave."—was held to be a valid holographic Will, bequeathing Gus' entire estate to the Red Cross. The holographic Will must always be signed, and the absence of a signature will bar a probate, even if there is conclusive proof of the handwriting of the testator and his testamentary intent. A holographic Will may not incorporate (see Chapter 3, Paragraph 19) any documents which do not meet the identical requirements of a holographic Will, and which are not written entirely in the hand of the testator. A joint holographic Will, signed by two or more persons, is a valid Will only for the person in whose handwriting the Will is written.

In a great many jurisdictions, notably those in which the civil law influence still leaves its mark, holographic Wills or those entirely in the handwriting of the testator are regarded differently insofar as the formalities of execution are concerned. A holographic Will is wholly in the testator's hand. It may not be typed, and a form may not be used in connection with the execution of a holographic Will. The code Napoleon specifically recognized holographic Wills, and exempted them from the usual formalities of execution, while in Virginia, up until 1750, witnesses were required only for Wills not entirely in the handwriting of the testator. Chart No. 4 shows the states and territories in which holographic Wills are recognized. Some states, however, though not recognizing holographic Wills executed within their own territorial jurisdiction, will nevertheless accept such a Will if it was valid in the jurisdiction of its execution. New York State recognizes holographic Wills only where executed by persons in actual military or naval service.

Holographic Wills are mentioned in this chapter not for the purpose of telling you how to make them, since you are cautioned not to make them, but to advise you to bring to your lawyer any holographis Will, or any paper resembling a holographic Will, which you may find. Your best friend, your great uncle, or business associate may have attempted to save a few dollars in lawyer's fees by making a holographic Will. You may read the first part of this book and feel that the paper stands no chance of being admitted to probate as a Will. Don't give up easily. Let your lawyer make the decision. What at first blush appears to be a rambling and incoherent letter may actually be a valid holographic Will. Do not attempt to make the decision yourself, anymore than you would want to be the judge of whether you require an immediate operation for appendicitis.

As a matter of caution, avoid holographic Wills. While some jurisdictions recognize them, if you attempt to use them, you invite trouble.

8. NUNCUPATIVE WILLS

A nuncupative Will is, in effect, an unwritten Will. It is not recognized in all jurisdictions, and wherever accepted, it is subject to strict requirements. A nuncupative or oral Will, in order to be recognized, must be made by a soldier or sailor in actual military service, or by a mariner while at sea. It is not necessary that the testator, either a soldier, sailor or mariner, be in immediate peril of death or in his last illness, though some states recognize oral Wills made by persons other than those in military service if the illness during which the Will was made actually results in death.

36

The oral or nuncupative Will ordinarily ceases to be valid one year after termination of the military service. If, however, the soldier or sailor should be incompetent, or should lack testamentary capacity at the expiration of one year from the date of his discharge, the nuncupative Will continues to be valid and enforcible until one year from the time the soldier or sailor shall have regained his testamentary capacity.

The nuncupative Will must be proved by the testimony of at least two witnesses, but it is not necessary for them to have been present at the same time. Two single declarations or statements of the soldier, sailor or mariner, if made to separate witnesses upon separate occasions, will be sufficient so far as the declarations are consistent, and are not at variance with the expressed testamentary intent, Statements by a sailor that if anything happened to him he wanted everything to go to his daughter, have been held a valid nuncupative Will. Two letters written by an American sergeant, one to his sister telling her that she was to have everything if anything happened to him, and another to his friend, stating that he wanted everything to go to his sister in the event that he "caught one some fine morning" were held sufficient to constitute a valid nuncupative Will, when shortly after the second letter, the expected event came to pass.

The extent to which a nuncupative Will will be recognized varies greatly from state to state. There are numerous jurisdictions in which nuncupative Wills are not recognized. Other jurisdictions limit the amount which may be bequeathed or devised under such a Will. In approximately one-third of the jurisdictions permitting such Wills, both real and personal property may be the subject of the Will, but in a number of states only personal property of a limited value may be bequeathed. If you have a problem involving a nuncupative Will, take it directly to a lawyer. He will know the requirements of your particular jurisdiction and will advise you whether a nuncupative Will may be probated. Above all, avoid making a nuncupative Will. At its best a nuncupative Will leads to litigation which is profitable to no one. Do not wait until you are ill, until you are in military service, or until you are at sea. Go to your lawyer immediately and your heirs will not be concerned and harassed by the problems of nuncupative Wills.

Chapter III

FORMS OF WILLS

1. GENERAL

Just as it is too late, after your death, to make a Will, or to decide how you want your property to be distributed, it is too late to explain just what you meant by the particular words and phrases which you employed in that very important document known as Your Will. When someone questions your intention, you will not be present to tell the Probate Court just what you wanted. It will be too late. Tell your lawyer what you want today and leave it to him to draw the Will. If you are a butcher, you know that you can trim a hind quarter and that your lawyer cannot. If you try to draw your own Will, you will undoubtedly meet with the same success or lack of success that would reward your lawyer's attempt to trim a hind quarter.

Study the Will clauses in this Chapter and point them out to your lawyer. Your consideration of these clauses, before consulting your lawyer, will make his work easier. If you do not see the appropriate clause, ask your lawyer to draft it for you.

2. HEADINGS OR CAPTIONS

Your lawyer will usually want to have some indication that the document is in fact your Will. To accomplish this purpose, he may have typed or written, at the beginning of your Will, or on the cover, the words (1) "My Will," (2) "Last Will and Testament of William Testator." These words are advisable but not strictly necessary.

3. INTRODUCTORY CLAUSES

The introductory clause of the Will serves the dual purpose of identifying you, and of establishing that you

39

are in fact executing and publishing your Will. The full name by which you are known should be used. Initials may, if desired, be used for middle names, but there should be at least one given name written in full, as well as your family name. Where you have changed your name, or have been known for some itme by another name, it is best to insert the words "formerly known as" or "also known as." The statement of your residence also serves to identify you. Typical introductory clauses are as follows:

(1) I, William Testator, of the City of Yonkers, County of Westchester, State of New York, do hereby make, publish and declare this to be my last Will and Testament.

(2) In the name of God, Amen. I, William Testator, of the City of Yonkers, County of Westchester, State of New York, enjoying good health and being of sound and disposing mind and memory but calling to mind the uncertainity of this life and willing to dispose of my wordly estate, do make and publish this my Last Will and Testament, committing my soul into the hands of my Heavenly Father, and trusting to His infinite goodness and mercy, and wishing to dispose of all the wordly estate wherewith it has pleased Almighty God to bless me in this life, I give, devise and bequeath the same in the following manner:

(3) In the name of God, Amen. I, Wiliam Testator, of the City of Reno, County of Washoe, State of Nevada, being of sound and disposing mind and memory, do hereby make, publish and declare the following as and for my Last Will and Testament.

(4) Where heading or caption "3" has been employed, it is possible, although not preferable, to employ the following introductory clause:

"My Will is as follows."

(5) I, Arthur H. Kelley, a legal resident of the State of California, now in active (military) (naval) (marine) (maritime) service in the United States (Army) (Navy)

40

(Marine Corps) (Merchant Marine) and having the (Army Serial Number   ) (Navy Serial Number   )
do hereby make, publish and declare this instrument to be my Last Will and Testament.

4. REVOCATORY CLAUSES

While a later Will which makes a total disposition of all of the testator's property revokes a previous Will, the general rule is that a later Will revokes an earlier Will only to the extent that the provisions of the two are inconsistent. Where there are inconsistent provisions, those of the later Will are controlling. To avoid the inference that you want any part of your earlier Will to remain in effect, your lawyer will insert a revocatory clause. It may be a simple clause such as:

(1) I hereby revoke all Wills and Codicils heretofore made by me, or (2) I hereby revoke all testamentary instruments heretofore made by me.

5. DEBTS AND FUNERAL EXPENSES

Your executor will have the power, and the obligation, to pay your debts and funeral expenses, even if you do not include a specific authorization. Your executor must use your assets to pay your debts and funeral expenses, and he must at the same time determine whether a debt is "just." You may not direct him to pay any particular creditor in preference to your other cerditors. The laws of each state establish the order of priority of your creditors. A typical and satisfactory clause is: I direct my executor to pay all my just debts and burial expenses as soon after my decease as may be practicable.

As a word of caution, if you have specific directions as to the conduct of your funeral, or as to where you want to be buried, it is best to keep a duplicate set of directions in a readily available place. Otherwise, there may be some delay in producing your Will, and you will probably be buried before your will is read and your wishes made known. If you are a veteran and want to be buried in Arlington National Cemetery, make the fact known to the persons closest to you. Your revelation of this very important wish may result in a considerable saving to your heirs, by removing the necessity for their purchasing that most expensive species of real estate, a cemetery plot.

6. GENERAL, SPECIFIC AND DEMONSTRATIVE LEGACIES

A General Legacy is a gift, payable out of the general assets of the estate, without regard to any particular fund or property. It does not require the delivery of any specific thing.

> I give and bequeath to my daughter, **Marion Carter,** the sum of Ten Thousand ($10,000) Dollars.

A Specific Legacy is a gift of a specified article, or a particular part of an estate, identified or distinguished in the Will from all others of the same nature. It is satisfied only by the delivery and receipt of the particular article bequeather. If you intend to make a legacy, describe in detail the article or articles which are to be the subject of your legacy. Be particularly careful in your description, as your failure to do so may involve your estate in litigation. Also remember in making such a bequest, that the legatee is entitled to receive the article only if it exists and is owned by you at the time of your death. (See Chapter 2, Sec. 6). If there is any possibility that you may not be the owner of the property at the time of your death, make an appropriate provision.

> (1) I give ad bequeath to my son, **Chester Chisholm,** the gold watch and chain which I inherited from my father, **Howard Chisholm.**

> (2) I give and bequeath to my son **Frederick Webster,** one hundred shares of the preferred stock of the Everlast Rubber Corporation, provided I shall be the owner of said stock at the time of my death.

(3) I give and bequeath to my wife, **Helen Testator**, any automobile of which I may be the owner at the time of my death.

A Demonstrative Legacy is in some ways a combination of the specific and general legacies. It provides for the payment of a certain amount of money, stock, or the like, payable out of a particular fund, or from a particular source, but also provides that if the particular fund or source named is insufficient, resort may be had to the general assets of the estate.

I give and bequeath to my friend, **Arthur Loyal**, the sum of Five Thousand ($5,000) Dollars to be paid from the proceeds of my royalties, and in the event that my royalties shall be insufficient to pay the said sum, I direct my executor to pay, from the general assets of my estate, such sum or sums as may be necessary to make up the difference between the actual amount of my royalties and the sum of Five Thousand ($5,000) Dollars.

In the case of a specific, general or demonstrative legacy, you must consider whether you want the legatee to receive the legacy, whether in personal property or in cash, free from the proportionate share of the estate taxes. If you do, be sure to tell your lawyer, so he can add to the legacy the words—

". . . free of all estate, transfer, inheritance and other taxes, of any nature."

Since you probably want your son to receive your watch, and your wife to have your automobile, without the payment of any estate taxes, you should call this to the attention of your lawyer. On the other hand, the legacies of several thousand dollars may be matters on an altogether different footing, where, in order to protect your residuary legatees, you have no desire to exempt the specific or general legatees of stock or cash from the payment of their proportionate share of taxes.

43

7. REAL ESTATE

Your Will is, for all practical purposes, a deed of all your real estate, taking effect at your death. This is true whether you describe the real estate by parcels, or whether you do not mention it specifically, and merely permit it to pass under the residuary clause of your estate. You should, however, describe the property in sufficient detail to identify it. If you own two houses on the same street, be sure that you have described each house with sufficient certainity to avoid any confusion—and do not be content with the street number, since it may be changed at any time. Remember that while you "bequeath" personal property and cash, you "devise" real property.

A clause devising real property reads, for instance, as follows:

"I give and devise unto my wife, Helen Testator, all of my real property situated in the Village of Irvington, Town of Greenburgh, County of Westchester, known as Tara's Halls."

When devising real estate, be sure to tell your lawyer just why you are making the specific devise. If you expect your devisee to occupy the real estate, you will probably want to add to the clause the words:

". . . together with all household furniture and other personal property used in connection therewith and situated thereon at my death."

You may desire to devise to your wife, or to some other relative, only the use of the real estate for her life, and, upon her death, to have the ownership pass to some other person or persons. Tell your lawyer about this, since you are getting into the field of trusts, one which is extremely complicated, and is sometimes difficult for even a lawyer to understand. One misstep may invalidate your carefully thought-out plans. Tell your lawyer what you want to do and leave the rest to him.

44

8. SURVIVORSHIP, COMMON DISASTER AND LAPSED LEGACIES

Suppose the person to whom you bequeath a substantial legacy dies before you. Ordinarily, the legacy will lapse, and instead of being paid into the estate of the legatee it becomes a part of your residuary estate. If your Will directs that Ten Thousand Dollars be paid to your son, John, and after John's funeral, you, yourself, die, without a chance to change your Will, the Ten Thousand Dollars will not pass to John's children, but will become part of your residuary estate. Some states have recognized the injustice of this rule, and have passed statutes directing that where the legatee (beneficiary) was a descendant, brother or sister of the testator, his death prior to that of the testator will not result in the lapse of the legacy, if the descendant, brother or sister shall be survived by a child or other descendant.

While these statutes which have given an added protection to the children of a deceased legatee make no distinction insofar as specific, general or demonstrative legacies, or devises, are concerned, they do not extend beyond the close relatives (descendants, brothers or sisters) of the testator. Most of the statutes, moreover, are so worded as to forestall the lapse of a legacy unless the testator specifically indicates that he wants the legacy to lapse if the legatee or devisee should precede him to the Pearly Gates. When you tell your lawyer about your legatees, he will ask you just how far you want your generosity to carry. You may be very fond of brother Tom, but rather contemptuous of his upstart son. Tell this to your lawyer, and he will draw a clause reading:

"I give and bequeath to my brother, **Thomas Brown**, if he survives me, the sum of Ten Thousand ($10,000) Dollars."

You feel differently about your brother Bill's family, and therefore you instruct your lawyer to draw the clause in this way:

"I give and bequeath the sum of Ten Thousand ($10,000) Dollars to my brother, William Brown, and, if he predeceases me, to his heirs."

Suppose, however, that your primary concern is your residuary legatee, and you want any lapsed legacies to become part of your residuary estate. Your lawyer will insert a provision in your residuary clause, giving the residue, "including lapsed legacies," to your residuary legatee, and you may then be assured that all legacies of predeceased legatees will lapse, regardless of their leaving surviving issue.

At this point you are probably wondering what happens if you and your wife die at or near the same time. It is best to make some provision for this contingency and to include a clause reading as follows:

"Should any beneficiary named herein die in the course of or as a direct result of the same accident, epidemic or other calamity as shall cause my death, then, and in that event, I give the bequest or devise allotted to him to such persons and in such manner and proportions as the same would have taken under the terms of this Will if said beneficiary had died before me."

If you include this clause, you, yourself, will still maintain control of your property. It will pass under your Will and not under the Will of your beneficiary. It is possible that you may not want this to happen. The beneficiary named in your own Will may be your wife or your son and you may feel that whatever disposition has been made in his or her Will will be satisfactory to you and that it is of little concern to you what bequests or devises have been made in the Will of your beneficiary. In that event, your clause will read as follows:

"Should any beneficiary named herein die in the course of, or as a direct result of the same accident, epidemic or other calamity as shall cause my death, I direct that

46

the bequest or devise allotted to him shall pass under the terms of his Will, or if he shall die intestate, under the laws of intestacy, in effect at the time and place of his death."

Discuss the question frankly with your lawyer. Have your wife or other beneficiary bring his or her Will to him to enable him to draw clauses which will accomplish your intent.

9. ENCUMBRANCES ON BEQUESTS OR DEVISES

If at the time of your death some article or personal property specifically bequeathed to a legatee is subject to a lien, mortgage, or other encumbrance, the legatee or devisee will take the property subject to such lien or mortgage and in the absence of a specific provision in your Will, will not be able to compel the executor to discharge the lien or mortgage from the assets of the estate. If your Will is that your legatee or devisee receive his legacy or devise free and clear, include a specific direction to that effect in your Will. Perhaps you want this provision to apply only to certain family heirlooms, such as that famous watch which you inherited from your father, or to the old family homestead. On the other hand, you may want to pass to your legatees or devisees, free from every encumbrance, a certain specific article which is not a part of your residuary estate. A clause covering your specific personal property is as follows:

"I bequeath to my son, John Testator, the gold watch which I inherited from my father and I direct that any liens or charges against said watch be paid out of the balance of my estate, and that my said son receive the watch free of any liens or charges."

If your home is the subject of your devise, your clause will read as follows:

"I give and devise to my wife my property known as Red Hill Farm in the County of Clallam, State of

Washington, free of any mortgage or charges thereon at the time of my death, and I direct that any mortgage or charges thereon be paid out of my personal estate in exoneration of the said premises."

These clauses apply only to specific devises or bequests. A general clause to cover all devises and bequests, except those comprising a residuary estate, is as follows:

"I hereby direct my executors to deliver to the devisees and legatees herein named all legacies or devises discharged of any liens or encumbrances of any nature whatsoever."

10. ADVANCEMENTS

As you talk over with your lawyer the provisions of your Will, you emphasize to him that you want to be fair. He asks you whether you want the money which you have loaned or advanced to a certain son or daughter to be considered as part of the share of your estate. Suppose, for instance, that you have already decided that your wife will receive two-thirds of your estate, and your four sons will divide the remaining one-third. How about that $3000.00 that you advanced to son John last year so he could build an addition to his house? Son Paul is several years younger than John, and he had no immediate need, but in another three or four years he, too, may need a larger house and you do not want him to suffer merely because he was born too late. You point this out to your lawyer, who then includes in your Will the following clause:

"I declare that all monies which I have or shall have advanced to any of my said children, or shall be owing to me from any of them at my decease, shall be considered as part of my residuary estate and shall be deducted from his, her or other respective shares."

On the other hand, suppose that son John has been exceptionally good to you. He has always gone out of his way to be considerate, and you feel that he actually deserves

48

a larger share of your estate. At the same time you do not want to offend your other children, so your lawyer inserts a clause reading:

> "I declare that such advancements as I may have made or hereafter make to any of my children (or to any person named in this Will) shall be in addition to, and not in satisfaction of any legacies, shares, portions, or other benefits given them under my Will."

Make a complete list of advancements and keep it with the Will. Do not include the list in your Will, since it will only complicate matters and since they may well be repaid before your death. Make a separate list and keep it with the Will, giving a copy to your lawyer or other executor.

11. RELEASE OF INDEBTEDNESS

If you would like to wipe out indebtedness owed to you, you can do this either by a specific provision in your Will referring to the particular debt or debts or by a general clause releasing and discharging any indebtedness owed to you at the time of your death. If you contemplate a release only of indebtedness existing at the time you execute your Will, it is best to refer to it specifically and to describe it in detail. A sample of this clause is as follows:

> "I release and forgive to my brother-in-law, William Gates, of Santa Barbara, California, the debt owed to me from him on account of money loaned and on which I hold his personal note dated January 6, 1946 in the amount $4000.000, together with accrued interest on same, and I direct my executor hereinafter named to mark the said note paid and cancelled, and to deliver it to the said William Gates."

You may realize that Bill will borrow more from you before your death or that he may repay this specific note and sign another one. If you desire to forgive any indebtedness

which may exist at the time of your death, your clause
will be as follows:

> "I hereby release my brother-in-law, William Gates,
> from the payment of any debts and interest thereon
> due me at the time of my death."

In releasing a debt you must not forget the ever-present
question of tax. The cancellation of an indebtedness may
be considered the equivalent of a legacy to the debtor in
the amount of the debt, and since it constitutes part of
your estate may be subject to State and Federal taxes.
If you do not want the debtor to pay his share of the
Estates Taxes, be sure to include a provision to that effect.
Your lawyer will select an appropriate provision similar
to one of those set forth in Paragraph 15.

12. PREFERRED LEGACIES AND
ABATEMENTS OF LEGACIES

If there is more than one person who is to benefit under
the terms of your Will, you undoubtedly have certain pre-
ferences among them. You probably want to be sure that
your wife is well provided for, and after you have taken
care of her you are more interested in your children than
in your friends and in the various charities which you have
named. You have complete freedom in providing for the
order of priority as long as you do not thereby disinherit
your wife or husband. The order of priority will always
be subject to the right of election unless that right is waived.
If you have provided for your wife in Paragraph-third
of your Will and for your children in Paragraph fifth, and
in various other paragraphs of your Will have made other
provision, your clause granting priority to your wife and
children will be as follows:

> "The legacies contained in Paragraphs Third and Fifth
> of this Will shall be entitled to preference in order
> in which they are set forth and shall be paid in full

50

before the payment of any other legacies, bequests or devises made in this Will."

Your financial situation at the time of your death may be altogether different from that existing at the time you planned and executed your Will. Realizing that your estimate of the size of your estate may differ radically from its valuation at your death, you should provide for the abatement or proportionate reduction of the various bequests. As a rule, you will provide that the bulk of your estate pass as a residue to the principal object of your generosity. The change in circumstances may be such that at the time of your death your residuary legatee will receive far less than the beneficiaries of specifis legacies or devises. To forstall such a situation, you may provide as follows:

"Any provision in this Will to the contrary notwithstanding, if the total of the legacies provided for in Paragraphs Seventh, Eighth and Ninth of this Will shall exceed ten per cent of the value of my estate passing under this Will, I direct that such legacies shall be abated proportionately, and the total payment made on account thereof shall not exceed ten per cent of my estate."

You may prefer to base your proportion upon specific amounts, but it will probably be to your advantage to use a percentage basis rather than to name figures. If you wish, your lawyer can combine your directions and can direct that the bequest shall not abate below a fixed figure.

If your Will is lengthy, and if you make numerous bequests and devises, you may actually set up a definite order of priority to govern the entire administration of your estate. Such a clause will be as follows:

"I direct that the legacies and bequests provided in this Will shall be paid in the following order, and that each class of legacy be paid in full before any payment to the succeeding class or classes:

1. Legacies to my children.

51

2. Legacies to my grandchildren.
3. Legacies to my friends or business associates.
4. Legacies to religious institutions, or
5. Other legacies."

13. DISINHERITANCE

For reasons best known to you, you may desire to disinherit your wife or your children or some other distributee who, in the absence of a Will, will be entitled to receive a share of your estate. Take the ordinary situation where you, as a person of moderate means, happily married, want everything to go to your wife. You have complete confidence in her ability to take charge of your assets and on her death, to distribute them to her children. You do not want to be hampered in her control of your assets. You will, therefore, add a clause as follows:

"I intentionally make no provision for my children, John and Helen."

This clause will successfully exclude John and Helen, and will permit your property to pass to your wife only if you and your wife do not have any more children. If a child should be born to you, or if you should adopt a child subsequent to the execution of your Will, the child will receive as share identical to that which would have passed to him if you had died intestate.(See Chapter 2, Paragraph 6E (2). You will, therefore, add after the names of your children the words "now living or any children hereafter born to or adopted by me."

One of your children may have done something of which you disapproved, or you may have advanced him money with the understanding that neither of you would ever mention the advance. You, therefore, wish to make some provision in your Will and do not wish to reveal the reason for your apparent discrimination. You may have absolute trust in Son John and feel certain that he will never contest your Will. On the other hand, John may die shortly after you, leaving a wife and minor children who may contest your Will with the utmost enthusiasm. For that reason, your lawyer may advise you to include the following clause:

> "The discrimination against my son John has been made with careful consideration of the welfare of all persons involved."

We discussed in Chapter One the extent to which you may or may not disinherit your husband or wife. We also pointed out that if your husband or wife has deserted you, the ordinary rules do not apply and you will be at liberty to proceed with such disinheritance. There may not be any question of a desertion. You may have made a settlement on your wife in lieu of her share in your estate as to her right to take against your Will, or you may have provided by a separation agreement that you each waive your rights to each other's estate. If this is the case, you should make such a statement to facilitate the task of your executor. Your clause will read:

> "I have no provision in this Will for my wife, Ann Testator, since she has waived her rights to any part of my estate by written instrument executed and acknowledged on the 18th day of January, 1947."

If your wife or husband has actually abandoned you and there has been a court order or decree separating you, you should not only provide a certified copy of the order or decree to be kept with your Will, but you should also refer to it with certainty. Your clause will then read:

> "Having been awarded a separation against my former wife, Ann Jones Testator, by decree of the Circuit Court of the County of Clallam, State of California, on the 17th day of January, 1947, it is my will that my said wife receive no part of my estate."

A more difficult problem is presented where there has been an abandonment, but no judicial determination that the

53

abandonment was with justification or was in effect an abandonment. Your clause will then be worded as follows:

"My husband, Irwin Jacobs, having abandoned me, it is my will that he receive no part of my estate."

An additional safeguard should be taken by the preparation of affidavits, not only by you, but by someone who, after your death, may be in a position to testify that there was in effect an abandonment. These affidavits should be executed and kept with the original Will

14. IN TERROREM CLAUSES

Suppose that your son Bill has always found himself in a position where he needed your help. You were glad to help him, but he and his wife did not show any appreciation. In disposing of your property, you want to distribute your legacies in such a way that discrepancies in your gifts to your children will be eliminated. At the same time, you know that Bill's wife, who is a little vixen, will kick up a terrible fuss if Bill receives a dime less than his brothers and sisters. Bill might take it as he should, but that wife of his will surely run to a lawyer and involve your estate in litigation. In order to guard against the possibility of objection to the probate of your will, your lawyer may insert a clause providing that any legatee who objects to the probate of the will forfeit his legacy.

The earlier rule, in force in the English Courts, was that such a clause did not affect a forfeiture of the legacy if there was in fact probable cause for contesting the probate. On the other hand, in the United States, there have been no cases holding that a testator may not, under any circumstances, impose upon the acceptance of his bounty a valid condition against an attack upon the validity of his Will. Beyond this point, however, the law varies from state to state, and it will be necessary for your lawyer to tell you the extent to which you may impose a condition. If, however, you impose such a condition, be sure that you provide for an alternate disposition or gift of the legacy or devise, since in a number of states the law is that a condition against contest is effectual when attached to a devise of real property, even without such a gift over, but that when such a condition is attached to a testamentary gift of personal property it is strictly "in terrorem" and is invalid unless there is a gift of the subject matter of the legacy to a third person in case of a contest, and forfeiture.

There are three rules which prevail in the United States:

(1) States which follow the English rule and hold that the penalty of forfeiture of interest imposed on a legatee or devise who attempts to contest the instrument will not be enforced when there were reasonable grounds for instituting the contest.

(2) States which allow such a provision where applied to a devise of real property, but do not permit it to defeat a legacy of personal property unless there is a gift of the subject matter of the legacy to a third person in the case of a contest.

(3) States which hold that a condition against contest, whether attached to a legacy or devise, is valid and enforceable whether there is a gift over, or not, and irrespective of the good or bad faith of the contest.

A typical clause, which may be used in the case of either real or personal property, is as follows:

"If any of the beneficiaries under this Will other than my wife, Ann Testator, shall object to the probate of this Will, or in any wise, whether directly or indirectly contest, or aid in contesting the same, or any of the provisions thereof, or the distribution of the whole, or any part of my estate thereunder, then, and in every such event, I annul any bequest herein made to such beneficiary, and it is my will that such beneficiary shall be absolutely barred and cut off from any share in my estate, and I direct that the said bequest or devise be part of my residuary estate."

After your lawyer has drawn the clause, you may ask why the words "other than my wife" were included. You may omit them if you wish, but remember that in most states you may not disinherit your wife, and by the same token, you may not provide for a forfeiture of her share in your estate to a figure below the minimum which your estate allows her.

15. ALLOCATION OF ESTATE TAXES

Every devise or bequest under a Will presents a question of the ultimate incidence of estate and inheritance taxes as between the residuary legatee and the beneficiaries under specific, general or demonstrative legacies, or devises of real estate. In New York, and in the majority of the other states of the Union, the Federal and State estate and inheritance taxes are required by law to be apportioned among all the legatees and devisees, unless the Will itself makes some provision to the contrary. In other states the contrary is true, and unless the Will contains a specific provision, all taxes will be paid out of the residuary estate. Your lawyer will know the law in your state, and will call it to your attention, to permit you to include the proper clause.

If your primary interest is in the payment of the individual legacies before the disposition of the residuary estate, your clause will be as follows:

"All estate, inheritance, transfer, succession and other death taxes and duties of any nature which may be assessed or imposed upon or with respect to the legacies or devises provided in and by the Will, shall be paid out of my residuary estate as an expense of administration without any appointment or probation."

If you say nothing in your Will, the payment of the taxes and their allocation will be governed by the law of the state of which you are a resident at the time of your death. The size of your estate is an important factor in arriving at this decision, since the tax rate increases in geometric proportion to the size of your estate. The legatee of cash or property in a large estate who is required to pay his share of the tax may receive substantially less than the legatee of a smaller estate, where the taxes are proportionately less. You may want to exempt some legatees, and let others pay their share. You probably want your wife and your children to receive their legacies free of any encumbrance, but how about your business associates, your charities, and your friends? If you are leaving a few miscellaneous legacies, and the residuary estate to your wife, you will probably include the following clause:

"I direct that each legatee and devisee named in this Will pay his proportionate share of any estate, transfer, succession or inheritance tax which may be assessed against my estate."

If your Will is that some, but not all, of the beneficiaries pay their proportionate share, your clause will be as follows:

"I direct that the legacies and devises in Paragraphs "Third" "Fourth" and "Seventh" of this Will be paid free of all estate, transfer, inheritance, and other death taxes, of any nature, and that all my other legatees and devisees pay their proportionate share of all estate, inheritance, and death taxes of any nature."

In drafting your tax clause, your lawyer will question you closely about property which, while not passing under your Will, may nevertheless be subject to taxes. The proceeds of insurance policies or the rights of the surviving tenant of a joint tenancy may be required to reimburse the estate for their portion of the taxes, if appropriate provisions are not made. (See Chapter Five).

16. CHARITABLE BEQUESTS AND DEVISES

As seen in Chapter One, there are several inquiries which must be made before you actually proceed with your charitable bequest. You must determine the correct name of the charity, its powers, whether it is incorporated, its ability to receive your gifts, and the adequacy of your gift for the purposes intended. Simple forms of bequests or devises to charitable, religious or fraternal organizations are as follows:

()1 "I give and bequeath the sum of five thousand ($5,000) dollars unto the Wilson Hospital, Inc., in the County of Los Angeles, State of California."

(2) "I give and devise unto Saint Peter's Home, Inc., a charitable corporation organized under the laws of the State of New York, my real estate located in the Village of Island Park, County of Nassau, State of New York."

When you earmark your gift for a specific purpose, do not forget that if the purpose fails, the courts may decide upon a substitute purpose, and this substitute purpose, while closely allied to that which you yourself have named, may not be one for which you had the same enthusiasm.

17. COMMUNITY PROPERTY CLAUSE

There is always the possibility that subsequent to the execution of your Will, you will move to one of the community property states, or, if you are not a resident, you may acquire or own property in such a state. To avoid misunderstandings, and to prevent any needless litigation, your lawyer, if he feels that there is any possibility of its necessitq, will include the following clause:

"In the event that any of my property at the time of my death is community property, under the laws of any jurisdiction, this Will shall be construed as referring only to my community interest therein."

18. CODICILS AND REVISIONS OF YOUR WILL

Just as your Will is not irrevocable, it is subject to revision at any time and should be examined periodically to determine whether any changes are necessary or advisable. Suppose, for instance, that at the time you made your Will, you lived in moderate circumstances, owned a small house, and by dint of good management, you somehow kept one good jump ahead of the sheriff. Shortly afterwards, however, that long awaited good break came along and being ready to take advantage of it, you found yourself amassing a considerable fortune. You were on your way to undreamed of riches, and before you knew it, you were a man of means. The first thing you did was to take out substantial insurance policies for your wife and children. A little later you bought a big house, and rented the small one. Then, one day at lunch, your lawyer, who had watched and helped while your fortunes prospered, said, "Jack, you should change your will. You're in a different position now than you were five years ago." He may also make this suggestion where your assets, instead of having increased, have shrunk, so that you are now less well off than when you made your original Will.

When you "change your Will," do you want to make an entirely new Will, or merely execute a codicil? A codicil, while a separate instrument, must be executed with all the formalities attending the execution of a Will. It does not revoke the Will, but merely supplements it and wipes out only those portions of the Will which are inconsistent with the codicil. Your lawyer will decide, when you tell him what you want to do, whether you should make an entirely new Will, or merely execute a codicil.

If the change which you desire is a simple one, such as the naming of a new executor, or the addition of one or more bequests, a codicil may be advisable. If, on the other hand, you want to revoke a legacy or a devise, it will be better for you to make an entirely new Will, and to destroy the old one. In such a case, the legatee or devisee named in the prior Will need not be notified after your death unless he is a person entitled to share in the estate in the event of intestacy. If he is notified, he will, of course, have an opportunity to contest the probate of your Will.

In some cases, however, your lawyer may advise the execution of a codicil instead of a new Will. If you are ill and you do not want to be burdened with an entirely new Will, or if there is some possibility that your competency to make a Will may be questioned, he may feel that there will be a greater possiblity of your wishes being carried out if you keep alive both the Will and the codicil.

A simple form of codicil is as follows:

"I, William Testator, of the County of Dade, State of Florida, do hereby make, publish and declare this codicil to be my Last Will and Testament, executed the 4th day of December, 1945:

First. I ratify and confirm my said Will in every respect, except insofar as the same is inconsistent with the provision of this codicil.

Second. I direct that my son, Thomas Testator, be substituted as my executor and trustee in place and stead of my son, John Testator, now deceased."
(Add Testimonium and Attestation Clauses. See Paragraph 23, Chapter Three.)

19. INCORPORATION BY REFERENCE

In most jurisdictions "Incorporation by Referenc" is permitted. A document which existed prior to the execution of the Will may be incorporated by reference into the Will, provided the Will itself specifically refers to it. In New York and in numerous other jurisdictions, no separate paper can ordinarily be incorporated into the Will, unless it is executed with the same formalities as the Will itself. Your lawyer will caution you to avoid such a procedure since it fails frequently to carry out your wishes, and may constitute an invitation to contest the Will or to litigate the distribution of property. In those jurisdictions where incorporation of some specific paper by reference thereto in the Will is permitted, the requirements are definite. The Will must refer to the writing to indicate that it has already been completed, and must evidence a clear intention to incorporate the writing into the Will.

The writing itself must be shown to correspond to the description in the Will and to have been in existence prior to the Will. A typical clause directing incorporation by reference is as follows:

"I direct my executor hereinafter named to distribute my jewelry and paintings in accordance with a sealed letter signed by me on December 25, 1925, and now in my safe deposit vault at the Emigrant Savings Bank, 17 East 57th Street, New York, New York."

If you intend to effect a distribution of specific articles by bequeathing them to a certain person and requesting that he dispose of them in accordance with separate instructions, you may be bequeathing your executor a considerable headache, since such instructions, while imposing a moral obligation, do not necessarily bind the legatee named, and may cause further trouble. If you feel that you can trust the particular legatee, give him the things outright and enclose a separate letter to him. If you feel that you can't trust him, don't put the property in his hands at all.

20. RESIDUARY CLAUSE

If you fail to complete your Will by neglecting to bequeath or devise all of your property, the state will complete the Will for you by distributing your undisposed property in accordance with the laws of intestacy prevailing in your state. To avoid such partial intestacy, your lawyer will include a residuary clause, which will dispose of all property not included in your specific, general, or demonstrative legacies or devises. You may want any specific bequests or devises whose beneficiaries predecease you to become part of your residuary estate (See Paragraph 8), along with any property which you have failed to mention. Your lawyer will then include the following clause:

"All property not hereinbefore disposed of, including

that bequeathed or devised to any person who shall predecease me, I give, devise, and bequeath to my wife, Ann Testator."

In your residuary clause you will make the provision for the principal object of your bounty. Since the welfare of your residuary legatee is your principal concern, your lawyer will point out the importance of providing for the allocation of taxes (Paragraph 15), preferred legacies and abatement of legacies (Paragraph 12). If you do not want to include an abatement clause, first make a substantial bequest to the person who is to be your residuary legatee, then, after proceeding with your residuary devises and legacies, direct that your residuary legatee receive the balance of your estate. By following this procedure, and by making the first bequest to your residuary legatee a preferred one, you can insure the residuary legatee a specific sum before any other legatees receive any benefits whatsover. After making such a provision, your residuary clause may be as follows:

"All the rest, residue and remainder of my estate, both real and personal, of every nature, and wherever situate, of which I may die seized or possessed, I give, devise, and bequeath of my wife, Ann Testator."

Your wife may be your principal concern, but what if she predeceases you? To provide for such a contingency, you may add the words:

". . . If she survives me, and if she does not survive me, to my surviving children in equal share."

21. PER CAPITA—PER STIRPES

As your children grow up, you become a grandfather many times over. Let us suppose that you have five children, and seventeen grandchildren, and one of your daughters, as well as your wife, has predeceased you. You decide that you want to leave the residue of your estate to your children and grandchildren, in equal shares. What do mean by "equal shares?" Do you mean five equal shares, seventeen equal shares, or twenty-one equal shares? And how about your still unborn grandchildren? If you want your surviving issue to take equal shares, you may provide that your residual estate pass to

". . . my surviving issue in equal shares, per capita."

This per capita provision will result in a counting of heads, and a subsequent division, giving each heir the same number of dollars and cents. If this is the distribution you want, be sure to tell your lawyer. If you do not provide for a per capita distribution to your issue, there will be a per stirpes distribution. If you either direct or permit a per stirpes distribution, and are survived by your son, John, and by three children of your deceased son, Tom, John will receive one-half, and each of Tom's children will receive one-sixth. Talk it over, and decide whether you want a per capita or a per stirpes distribution.

22. EXECUTORS, GUARDIANS AND POWERS

Your executor must be of full age, although you may name a corporation. A close relative is usually best and your husband or wife will be the ideal person to administer your estate. Your executor will need the assistance of an attorney and it may be well for you to give some consideration to naming your attorney as co-executor, particularly if he has been your attorney for a long time and is as close to you and your affairs as your old family doctor. Your surviving husband or wife will, of course, be the guardian of all your children who are under 21 and unmarried, but you should make some provision for guardianship in the event that you and your wife die at the same time, or in the event that she predeceases you.

Unless you include a provision exempting your executor from the necessity of posting a bond, in most states he will be required to post security with the court for the faithful performance of his duties. Your executor should be some person in whom you have sufficient confidence to dispense with this requirement. If your trust in him is so limited that you feel a bond is necessary, you should look further for an executor. A bond not only entails additional expense but additional work as well, since bonding companies insist upon being notified of every step taken, and upon the right to countersign all checks.

If you are worried about his surviving you or about his ability to continue in his position of responsibility after several years, you may consider naming your lawyer, or a bank or trust company as co-executor, if your estate is of sufficient size to warrant the added expense. A simple form of appointment of executor is as follows:

"I nominate, constitute, and appoint my wife, Ann Testator, as executrix of this Will, and I direct that no bond or other security be required from her for the faithful performance of her duties."

In the event that your wife should predecease you or in the event that she should be unwilling or unable to assume the responsibilities, you may make provision in your Will for a substitute executor. Your clause would then read:

"I nominate, constitute, and appoint my wife, Ann Testator, as executrix of my Will, and as substitute executor I appoint my brother, Alfred Testator, and direct that no bond or other security be required from either my executrix or my substitute executor."

Just how much authority do you want your executor to have? Do you want to permit him to "do or perform any act which I myself might do, if living," or do you want to limit him to certain specific acts? Do you, for instance, want him to carry on your business? Suppose you own a small but prosperous grocery store. Under the law in almost all jurisdictions, your executor or trustee will be required to sell your interest in the grocery store and to invest the proceeds in "legal" investments which are limited to certain specific types of securities, usually considered much safer, but with a much lower return. If you want him to

64

continue to hold your interest in the grocery store, or in any other specific property or business, it will be necessary for you to include a retention clause which your lawyer will draft in substantially the following terms:

"I hereby give and grant to my executor and trustee or his successor or successors, power and authority to hold and retain all or any part of my estate, or any trust created thereby, in the form in which the same may be at the time of my decease or at the time of the receipt thereof by my said executor for as long a time as he may deem advisable."

If you name a business associate, be careful to enumerate his powers, since you may run into the problem of conflicting interests, and he may find himself hamstrung and unable to act without extensive delay and expense. Discuss this with your lawyer who will be familiar with the law in your particular jurisdiction and who will draw the proper clause.

Do you want your executor to convert everything into cash, and then make his distribution, or are you willing to let him take a distribution in kind? If you want him to have the option to make a distribution in kind, to forestall the possibility of a forced sale in an unfavorable market, and at the same time to permit a prompt distribution to your heirs, your lawyers will include the following clause:

"I hereby authorize and empower my said executor by way of due and full performance of his duties and obligations to assign, transfer and deliver in kind any property of whatsoever nature, whether received, purchased, or acquired by my executor."

You may have unbounded faith in your executor's financial ability and acumen. If you have such confidence in him, give him the power to invest and reinvest and include in your Will the following clause:

"I hereby give and grant to my executor the power to invest and reinvest any funds in my estate or any trust created hereby, without being limited to investments authorized by law for trust funds."

Your executor or trustee will still be required to exercise a sound discretion and business judgment, and he will still be required to report to the court at regular intervals. Give him the power to sell when he feels that the market is best. Empower him to

"... sell, exchange, partition, or otherwise dispose of any property, real or personal, of which I may die seized or possessed, or which may at any time form part of my estate or any trust created hereby, at public or private sale for such purposes and upon such terms, including sales on credit, in such manner, and at such prices as he may determine."

Give him the power to borrow, since your death may occur at a time when the market is at its lowest, and he may require ready cash to pay debts, or estate and inheritance taxes. Do not force him to sell in an unfavorable market, but let him borrow money, if necessary, to pay estate taxes and to discharge mortgages or liens upon your property. Give him the power to

"... borrow money for any purpose in connection with the administration of my estate."

Let him make any settlements, or adjust claims without having to run to court for permission, and if you have sufficient confidence in him, permit him to defer calling in any debts. Give him power to

"... defer and postpone the required payment of any debt which may be owing to me from (a specific person) (or any debt in general) at the time of my decease, for such period as he may deem advisable (but not exceeding one year or two years)."

The details can be worked out by you with your attorney, and will depend upon your own particular circumstances. You should also give him the power to

> ... adjust, settle, compromise and arbitrate claims or demands in favor of or against my estate upon such terms as he may deem advisable."

Unless he is a superman, he will need some help. Give him the specific power to

> "... retain attorneys, accountants, custodians, counsel, and such other persons as he may deem advisable in the administration of my estate and to make such payments therefor as he may deem reasonable."

If your executor is of sufficient responsibility, you need not worry about his going overboard on the question of expenses. He will still be subject to the supervision of the court, and he must be reasonable.

There may be some specific act which you wish to authorize. Talk it over with your lawyer and, between the two of you, you will have no difficulty in working out a clause which will accomplish your purpose and will nevertheless be legally sufficient.

23. TESTIMONIUM AND ATTESTATION CLAUSES

At the end of the Will, your lawyer will insert the testimonium clause which will be substantially as follows:

> "In Witness Whereof, I have hereunto set my hand and seal this 3rd of March, 1937.

There is no specific clause for this form, and it varies within somewhat narrow limits. Your lawyer will usually include the word "Seal" because some jurisdictions still require a seal. He may word the testimonium clause as follows:

> "In Witness Whereof, I sign, seal publish, and declare this as my Last Will and Testament in the presence of the persons witnessing it at my request this 3rd day of March, 1947"

and if your Will is or more than one page, he may include
the number of pages in both the testimonium clause, and in
the attestation clause. Such a form of testimonium clause
may be:

"In Witness Whereof, I have, to this my Last Will and
Testament consisting of five pages, subscribed my name
and fixed my seal this 3rd day of March 1947"

After you yourself have signed the Will, your witnesses
will sign, and you will require an attestation clause for
them. A simple clause is as follows:

"Signed, sealed, published, and declared by Julian
Dickerson, the testator above named, to be his Last
Will and Testament in our presence, and we, at his
request, and in his presence and in the presence of
each other, have hereunto subscribed our names as
witnesses this 3rd day of March 1947.

.... residing at ....

.... residing at ....

.... residing at ....

If your Will is longer than one page, the same statement
of the number of pages may be included, and the Attestation clause may read as follows:

"Signed and declared by the said Julian Dickerson as
and for his Last Will and Testament, consisting of five
pages, in the presence of us (all of us being present
at the same time) who, at his request, and in his presence and in the presence of each other, have hereunto
subscribed our names as witnesses this eleventh day
of November, 1944."

If you are blind, or if you are unable to read, and the
Will must be read to you, your lawyer will include such

a statement in the attestation clause to insure the probate of the Will, in the event of any contest.

24. FORMS OF COMPLETE WILLS

(a) Simple Will of Married Man leaving all property to wife.

"I, Walter Vantangeln, of the County of Dade, State of Florida, being of sound and disposing mind and memory, do hereby make, publish, and declare the following as and for my Last Will and Testament, hereby revoking all wills made by me at any time heretofore and appointing my wife, Susie Vantagelin, as executrix, without bond.

First: I direct my wife, Susie Vantangeln, to pay all my just debts and funeral expenses as soon as practical.

Second: I give, devise, and bequeath all my estate, of whatsoever nature and wheresoever situate, unto my wife, Susie Vantangeln, absolutely and forever.

Third: I direct that this Will remain in full force and effect, notwithstanding the subsequent birth of issue to me and my said wife, Susie Vantangeln.

In Witness Whereof, I have hereunto set my hand and seal this 19th day of March, 1945.

....

Signed, sealed, published, and declared by the said Walter W. Vantangeln, as and for his Last Will and Testament in the presence of us and each of us, who, at his request and in his presence and in the presence of each other, have hereunto subscribed our names as witnesses.

.... **residing at** ....

.... **residing at** ....

.... **residing at** ....

(b) Simple Will of Wife leaving all property to husband
and children in the event he predeceases her.

I, Frances Webster, of the City of Slowburg, State of
Illinois, being of sound and disposing mind and memory, do hereby make, publish, and declare the following as and for my Last Will and Testament, hereby
revoking all testamentary instruments heretofore executed by me and appointing my husband, Frederick C.
Webster, as my executor without bond.

First, I direct my executor to pay my just debts and
funeral expenses as soon after my decease as may be
practical.

Second, I give, devise, and bequeath unto my husband,
Frederick C. Webster, all my property of whatsoever
nature and wheresoever situate, in fee simple. In making this disposition of my property, I am not unmindful
of the welfare of my children, Frederick C. Webster,
Jr. and Marjorie Webster, and I desire this Will to remain in full force and effect, notwithstanding the subsequent birth of issue to me and my. husband.

Third, In the event that my husband shall predecease
me, I give, devise, and bequeath all of my estate to
my surviving issue in equal shares per stirpes, and I
direct that Walter Vantangeln serve as my substitute
executor and guardian of my surviving minor issue and
that no bond or other security be required for the faithful performance of his duties.

In Witness Whereof, I sign, seal, publish, and declare
this my Last Will and Testament in the presence of

70

the persons witnessing it at my request on the 10th
day of October, 1944.

....

The foregoing Will was signed on October 10, 1944,
subscribed, sealed, published, and declared by the
testatrix as her Last Will and Testament in our presence, and in the presence of each other, who subscribe
our names as witnesses, the Will having been read aloud
to us by the testatrix immediately after she signed the
Will, and this attestation clause having been read aloud
to us in her presence, all of us, including the testatrix,
being present together, throughout the execution and
attestation of the Will.

..........................residing at ....

..........................residing at ....

..........................residing at ....

(c) Will of Unmarried Person

I, Herbert Williams, of the Town of Columbia, County
of Ashford, State of Pennsylvania, being of sound and
disposing mind and memory, do hereby make, publish, and declare the following as and for my Last Will
and Testament.

First, I hereby revoke all Wills heretofore made by me
at any time.

Second, I direct my executor hereinafter named to pay
my just debts and funeral expenses as soon after my
death as may be practical.

Third, I give, devise, and bequeath all of my estate of
whatsoever nature and wherever situate, to my mother,
Helen Williams, and if she predeceases me, to my

71

father, Thomas Williams, and if he predeceases me, to my brother, George Williams.

Fourth, I nominate, constitute, and appoint my brother, George Williams, as the executor of this my Last Will and Testament.

Fifth, I direct that no bond or other security be required of my executor or substitute executor.

In Witness Whereof, I sign, seal, publish, and declare this as my Last Will and Testament in the presence of the persons witnessing it at my request this 11th day of November, 1944.

....

Subscribed by the testator in the presence of each of us and at the same time declared by him to us to be his Last Will and Testament, thereupon, we, at his request and in his presence and in the presence of each other, signed our names as witnesses this 11th day of November, 1944.

.... residing at ....

.... residing at ....

.... residing at ....

(d) Will of a Married Man providing for a specific and general bequest but making primary provision for wife.

I, Claude Gaffney, of the City of Tilton, State of New Hampshire, do hereby make, publish, and declare the following as and for my Last Will and Testament, hereby revoking all Wills and Codicils made by me at any time, and directing that my executrix, or substitute executor, serve without bond.

First, I nominate, and appoint my wife, Leila M. Gaff-

72

ney, as executrix of this my Last Will and Testament, and direct that she pay my funeral expenses and just debts as soon after my decease as may be practical.

Second, I give and bequeath to my wife the sum of $50,000 free of any estate, succession, or inheritance taxes, and I further direct that this legacy be paid in full before the payment of other legacies or bequests under this Will.

Third, I give and bequeath to each of my children, Harold Brusher Gaffney, Leonard Davis Gaffney and Willard Gaffney, the sum of $5000.00 each.

Fourth, I give and bequeath to my friend, Kaspar Butnes of Wilmington, Delaware, the gold watch given to me by the members of my battery during my service in the United States Army, and direct that the said watch be delivered to him free and clear of all estate and inheritance taxes and liens of any nature whatsoever.

Fifth, I bequeath to the Penrod Welfare Fund, Inc., a charitable corporation organized under the laws of the State of Louisiana, sum of $50.00.

Sixth, I bequeath to the Seafarers Society, Inc., a membership corporation organized under the laws of the State of Lousiana, the sum of $50.00.

Seventh, All the rest, residue, and remainder of my estate of whatsoever nature and wheresoever situate, I give, devise, and bequeath to my wife, Leila Gaffney, in fee simple, and in the event my said wife should predecease me, or in the event that we shall die as a result of the same catastrophe or epidemic, I direct that the residue of my estate be distributed among my surviving issue in equal shares per capita.

In Witness Whereof, I have hereunto set my hand and seal on this ....day of June, 1949.
Signed and declared by the said Claude Gaffney as and

for his Last Will and Testament in the presence of us, who at his request, in his presence, and in the presence of each other, have hereunto subscribed our names as witnesses.

.... residing at ....

... . residing at ....

.... residing at ....

25. THE MARITAL DEDUCTION

Beginning with the Revenue Act of 1948, married couples in non-community property states were afforded equal opportunity to leave to a surviving spouse half of the gross estate on a tax-free basis. As you have seen from previous discussion, this operates automatically in community property states since, but for precise exceptions to which the husband and wife themselves agree, each is deemed to hold an undivided half of all property they own. On death, therefore, each owns only one-half of the community property, and only that half is calculable in the estate of a deceased marital partner.

In non-community property states, the popularity of the so-called marital deduction Will has established it within the last generation as the rule, rather than the exception. The simple-form Wills, such as those previously described are adequate, as tools of estate planning, only for very modest estates of less than $60,000. ($60,000 is the personal exemption, and any estate below this amount is not only free of estate tax, but there need not be an estate tax filing).

The marital deduction operates simply. A husband simply bequeathes to his wife, for example, either assets that are calculated to reflect one half of his gross estate, or adopts a fractional formula for stating the bequest. When one considers, as will be demonstrated in the upcoming section on Trusts, that many assets may be left by the operation of instruments other than Wills -- a life insurance policy, a joint bank account, a trust -- some or all of which assets may be part of the estate, but not passing under the Will -- the fractional formula is frequently selected by attorneys as creating the greatest flexibility. But it must be used with care, as there are likely to be specific assets that the husband intends the wife to have, and would not want those assets in any other hands. If, for example, it is intended that a wife carry on a business, the husband must be sure to bequeath to the wife sufficient stock in the business to enable her to control it.

26. WORDING THE MARITAL DEDUCTION

A typical marital deduction bequest, embodying the fractional formula, would be as follows:

"I give and bequeath to my wife, MABEL MERCER, a fractional share of my estate, which shall be equivalent to the amount of the maximum marital deduction obtainable in fixing the federal estate tax upon all of the items included in my gross estate for federal estate tax purposes (whether or not passing under this Will or included in my estate for purposes of actual probate). There shall be subtracted from such fractional share any property passing to my wife outside probate, which qualifies for the marital deduction. The valuation placed upon the property in the estate in finally settling my estate tax liabilities shall determine such fractional share."

This clause is usually well accompanied by the following:

"The foregoing bequest shall be paid only in assets which qualify for the marital deduction, and no state inheritance or federal estate taxes shall be paid from or charged against property passing by virtue of this bequest."

And, the following:

"In selecting specific items of property from my estate for final distribution, my executor shall distribute property which has appreciated in value or depreciated in value, since my death, in such a manner that the benefits arising to, and detriments suffered by the estate with respect to such changes in value shall be equally apportioned by value among my beneficiaries not receiving cash bequests."

27. DANGER OF DIMINISHING THE MARITAL DEDUCTION

Both testator and his attorney must be aware of diminishing the value of the marital deduction by bequests or provisions that have the effect of leaving the wife with less than half the estate. For, to the extent that what a surviving spouse is left is less than half the estate, the marital deduction is lost, and the taxes will be greater. If, for example, a husband wants to leave a business to a son, but the business is the major asset in the estate, if he leaves the business to the son, he will lose the greater part of the marital deduction.

Many husbands likewise fear the possibility that a wife may not be able to handle money or property. They, therefore, balk at making an outright bequest to the wife, beyond a stipulated sum of money. But there are ways of handling this. A marital deduction trust can be set up, providing income for the wife for her life, and giving her a power of appointment as to who will be her successor beneficiary. Combined with powers to invade the corpus for her benefit, this method can effectively assure the marital deduction, while placing the assets beyond the outright reach of the wife.

So, in the case of the business as the major asset, shares of stock can be left to the wife in trust, with the son, as trustee, and a power of appointment in the wife to name the ultimate beneficiary. By so apportioning the shares as to assure that the son's own holdings are always sufficient to operate the business, the marital deduction is rescued, while continuity of the business in designated hands is assured.

28. THE TESTAMENTARY TRUST

A marital deduction trust is in effect a testamentary trust, in that it is created by the Will of the testator. It is distinguished, as we shall see, from inter vivos trusts -- those created by an individual while he is alive.

The testamentary trust is normally identified, however, with the second half of an estate -- that segment of the estate which is outside the marital deduction, and on which estate taxes will be payable. The use of such a trust is indicated where a testator's desires are the reverse of what is described above. Assume, for example, that a husband wants to leave everything he owns to his wife. The immediate tax consequences are the same as if he left her half the estate and left half the estate to others. Half of the estate will pass to her tax-free; and the other half will be taxable (net of the personal exemption of $60,000.)

It is at the wife's death, however, that the problem of a second levy of taxes creates a threat. Generally, if a wife's death follows early · on a husband's (or vice-versa), there is a credit for taxes that have been paid on the estate of the deceased spouse. This credit graduates downward, however, with the result that if the wife outlives the husband by ten years, what she leaves at her death is fully taxable. Thus, if a man leaves everything to his wife, at her death, everything that she passes to her beneficiaries will be taxable, if she has outlived him for ten years. If we assume, for example, that she will leave everything to her children, then the additional tax has become a needless and expensive step.

The husband, in his Will, can create a trust (trusts, actually) naming each child as an ultimate beneficiary of the trust for that child. Life income from each and all trusts can be reserved to the wife, including the power to invade the corpus for the benefit of the wife. Thus, although the wife actually has virtually all the rights in the assets that she would have if she were left them outright, the fact that she is only an income beneficiary, with no right to name the ultimate beneficiaries, avoids the assets coming into her estate. At her death, they pass to the children under the husband's will, and no estate tax is due, since they are not part of the wife's estate.

29. WORDING THE TESTAMENTARY TRUST

The following is a typical formulation of a testamentary bequest in trust, after either an outright bequest or marital deduction trust has assured the availability of the marital deduction.

"All the rest and residue of my estate, I bequeath to my trustees, as hereinafter named, for the purposes and upon the terms and conditions following:

(a) The trustee shall pay the net income derived from the trust estate to, or use and apply the same for the benefit of my wife, MABEL MERCER, as long as she shall live.

(b) The principal of this trust may be distributed to or for the benefit of my wife at any time or times to the extent that in the sole judgment and discretion of the trustees, such distribution is necessary for her health, education, support or other expenses of maintenance, including a reasonable number of the luxuries of life. Payments of such sums shall not create rights in any other person under this Will, and such payments need not be restored to the corpus of the trust estate.

(c) Upon the death of my wife, the trustees shall divide the entire estate into as many shares of equal market value as there shall be children of mine then living, and shall set aside and designate one such share as a separate trust fund for the benefit of each living child of mine. I declare that as of the date of this last Will and Testament, I have now a son, ARTHUR, and a daughter, CONSTANCE.

78

So much of the net income and principal from each trust described shall be paid to or for the benefit of the child for whose benefit the trust is held, as in the sole discretion and judgment of the trustees is necessary and proper for his or her welfare. Income not distributed shall be added to principal.

As each child attains the age of 25, one half of the trust for that child shall be distributed to him; and at age 30, the remaining half of the trust for that child shall be distributed to him. If any child shall die before the distribution herein set forth, the principal and accumulated income in such trust shall be delivered over to the trust for the surviving child, and shall be governed by the provisions then applicable to that trust."

OR

"(c) Upon the death of my wife, the trustees shall divide the entire estate into as many shares of equal market value as there shall be children of mine then living, and shall forthwith distribute each such share to each such living child. I declare that as of the date of this Last Will and Testament, I have now a son, ARTHUR, and a daughter, CONSTANCE."

It will be noted that under the first formulation of (c), it is assumed that the children may still be minors at the death of the wife, and therefore, the continuation of the trust. Under the second formulation, it is assumed that the children are mature adults and capable of managing their own property.

30. COMMON DISASTER

If the reader will review the language cited at page 50, he will note that two alternatives are given. Under the first, if a husband and wife die in common disaster, or under circumstances where it is difficult or impossible to ascertain who died first, the husband is deemed to have survived the wife. This alternative does not generally make sense where the marital deduction is involved. The second alternative cited does a better job from the standpoint of tax consequences.

For, under the first alternative, all of the estate passes to the children, without any benefit of the marital deduction. The only exemption is the personal exemption of $60,000. If, however,

79

the wife is presumed to survive the husband, half of the estate passes to the wife tax-free, while the other half passes directly to the children, net of the personal exemption. Then, on the premise that dual wills have prepared for husband and wife, to integrate with each other, the portion which has passed to the wife tax-free now passes to the children under her will, net of her personal exemption. Minimally, an additional $60,000 of exemption has been made available. Additionally, each estate, being smaller, the taxes to be paid on each are considerably reduced.

31. THE PREPARATION OF INTEGRATED WILLS

The previous discussion underscores the need for a husband and wife to draw wills simultaneously, and arranged to integrate with each other, so that their joint intentions can be assured. In general, on the premise that the wife's estate, if she dies first, may be minimal, her will need not be concerned with a division of her property, and she may, without tax consequence, leave everything to her husband, if that is her desire. (This does not apply, of course, where the wife is herself a substantial property owner). If she survives her husband, the provisions should integrate with the husband's treatment of his residuary estate, so that regardless of who survives whom, the joint intentions of the couple are realized.

Chapter IV

ADMINISTRATION OF ESTATES

1. PROBATE

John Testator is dead. Shortly after his passing there is a reading of his Will. There is no requirement that there be such a reading, but sooner or later the executor, upon finding the Will, must notify the persons interested. It may be that John has placed his Will in a safe deposit vault, and has given no one access to the vault. In that case it will be necessary to obtain a court order permitting the opening of the vault. A representative of the State Tax Commission will be present to see that nothing is removed except the Will, which is then sent to the Surrogate's, Probate, or Orphans' Court of the county in which the testator was resident at the time of his death. The executor named in the Will then asks the court to appoint him, and to issue, under the seal of the court, letters testamentary evidencing his appointment and his authority as executor.

All persons interested must be notified that the Will has been filed. Any person who would be entitled to any share of the estate, if there were no Will, is a person interested, and jurisdiction of him must be obtained before the Will can be probated. If there is no objection, as is usual in probate cases, the interested parties will sign a "waiver and consent" that the Will be admitted to probate. If they do not consent, they must be served with a "citation" either personally or by publication. The citation is similar to a summons and is issued by the court directed to the interested parties and advising them of the date on which the Will will be offered for probate. Sometimes it is served personally, but in the event that the interested party lives abroad, or in some far distant or inaccessible place, or if his address is unknown, it may be less expensive and more expeditious to have him served by publication. In that case, the court orders that a copy of the citation be published in various newspapers, and if the address of the interested party is known, that a copy be mailed to him.

He is then given a specified number of days to object to the probate of the Will, and if he does not object, the witnesses to the Will will be called to the Surrogate's Court, will identify the signatures on the Will, and testify to the circumstances of its execution. The affidavits referred to in Chapter Two will be used at this point.

If any of the interested parties are displeased with the contents of the Will, they have the right to object to its probate and to demand a hearing of their objections.

The grounds upon which a Will may be contested and the circumstances involved are as follows:

(a) **Due Execution of the Will.** If the formalities requisite to the execution a Will have not been complied with, the Will must be denied probate. If the testator failed to declare the instrument as his Will, or if he neither signed the Will in the presence of the witnesses nor acknowledged to them his signature on the Will, then the instrument may not be admitted to probate for lack of due execution.

(b) **Testamentary Capacity.** The testator will be presumed to have had sufficient capacity to execute his Will.

(c) **Undue Influence.** The test of undue influence is:

"Was the influence sufficient to destroy free will?" To satisfy this test, the influence must necessarily vary with the strength or weakness of the mind of the testator. Influence, which might be patently insufficient to change the mind and affect the volition of a vigorous testator of thirty-five or forty, may have been more than sufficient to affect a failing man in his seventies or eighties. Undue influence is a question of fact and must actually be sufficient to destroy a man's free will. The fact that a testator acted in an immoral manner does not mean that he was subject to undue influence. As long as he did what he wanted to do, the instrument is his Will and will be admitted to probate.

82

(d) Fraud and Forgery. The same elements of fraud must be shown as in any civil action, but the amount of proof required is usually somewhat greater in Will cases.

(e) Revocation. This may involve not only proof of the execution of a subsequent instrument, but actual destruction and intent of a testator that the destruction constituted a revocation.

The proponent of the Will has the burden of proof on the issues of due execution and testamentary capacity. The burden of proof is on the contestant on issues of undue influence, fraud and revocation.

It should be noted that the only persons who can contest the probate of a Will are those who have something to gain if the Will is not probated. Consequently, the power to enter a contest is not limited to next of kin, and persons who would take if there were an intestacy, but may be extended to legatees or devisees of a prior Will who would be entitled to take as beneficaries under the prior Will if a subsequent Will should fail to be admitted to probate.

After the objections have been heard, or if there are no objections, after the witnesses to the Will have testified, the Surrogate or Probate judge, if he is satisfied that the testator was competent, and that the formalities of execution were duly complied with, will sign a decree admitting the Will to probate and will issue Letters Testamentary to the executor, permitting him to exercise the powers granted under the Will.

2. INTESTACY AND ADMINISTRATION

If you die without a Will, the State will, in effect, make a Will for you by providing for distribution of your assets among your heirs at law. Someone will be appointed to act as your administrator or administratix, and a bond will always be necessary. In the appointment of your administrator, preference will be granted in the following order—1) surviving husband or wife, 2) children, 3) grand-children, 4) father or mother, 5) brothers or sisters, and 6) any other next of kin entitled to share in the distribution of the estate.

If no other next of kin can be found, the court will usually appoint the Public Administrator. Persons under 21 years of age, incompetents, aliens who are not residents of the State, or persons convicted of a felony may not serve as administrators. All persons entitled to share in the estate must be notified of the application for appointment. Bitter contests sometimes develop between warring factions of a family and there is no more disconcerting spectacle than groups of brothers and sisters aligned against each other in the administration of the estates of their parents. This is a most compelling argument for the prompt preparation and execution of your Will. After a hearing has been held and a bond filed, the Surrogate will appoint the best quali-fied and most closely related applicant as administrator. From that point on, the proceedings are identical with those of probate.

3. TRANSFER OF ASSETS AND TAX ASSESSMENTS

After the Letters have been granted, the executor or administrator must collect the assets of the estate. The first thing he must do is ascertain the identity and location of all the property of the decedent, and take the appropriate steps to obtain possession. He will require waivers from the State Tax Commission, and must list each item for which he desires a waiver. After the Tax Commission consents to the transfer of the property to the estate or to the individual legatee, the waiver will be served upon the person or cor-poration holding the property and it will then be trans-ferred. Corporations usually refuse to transfer their stock without a copy of Letters Testamentary or Letters of Ad-ministration and a tax waiver, and some corporations also require an affidavit as to the status of the estate. Title to real property is transferred by recording in the office of the County Clerk or Register a certified copy of the will.

84

When all assets have been collected, the executor or administrator files his inventory with the State Tax Commission, and an appraiser is appointed. The appraiser may require some assistance in the valuation of jewelry, clothing, works of art and other specific items, but will, as a general rule, accept the market value of stocks and other securities. After the appraisal is completed, the Surrogate or Probate Judge will sign an order fixing the estate tax. The executor, however, need not wait until the order is signed before paying the estate tax. In most states, he may pay it immediately upon or shortly after death, and he will thereupon be entitled to a discount. Lawyers usually make a payment as soon as the executor or administrator is appointed, obtain a temporary receipt, and then after the tax has been finally determined by the Court, apply for a refund of the balance if the tax has been overpaid.

The Federal tax is determined by the Bureau of Internal Revenue, and determinations as to value made in State proceedings are not conclusive upon the estate or the Government. In connection with the assessment of the taxes, your lawyer may find it advisable to retain the services of an accountant.

4 THE ACCOUNTING

After the taxes have been paid, the executor or administrator must turn his attention to the payment of bills and charges against the estate. Before making any distribution to legatees, he will usually satisfy himself that the estate is solvent and that there are sufficient assets to pay the bills. He will pay all bills, pay the taxes, and then proceed with the distribution of the assets of the estate, either as directed by the Will or, if there was no Will, as directed by law. After he has made his distributions, he will file his account and ask the Court to approve it. All interested persons will then receive a further citation, and will be required to show the Court some valid reason why the account should not be accepted as submitted, and why the executor or administrator should not be discharged from any further responsibility. If, however, the executor or administrator fears litigation, and fears that no distribution made by him will satisfy all parties, he may retain certain of the assets, and in his accounting, ask the Court to direct further distribution. It is on this accounting proceeding that the right of election and its extent will be determined. The Court will accord a full hearing, and may, in an accounting proceeding, have any number of lawsuits to decide at one time. If the executor does not pay a claim against the estate and feels that it is wise he will issue a citation to to the creditor advising him of the filing of the account and putting him on notice that he must state his objections and show why he should be paid .

If the Court is satisfied that the distribution made by the executor or administrator is proper, a decree will be signed discharging him from further responsibility, and granting him his commission as such executor or administrator. If the Court is not satisfied, it may direct the executor or administrator to make good any unauthorized or improper expenditure or distribution, and may direct the future or final distribution.

If, however, everyone agrees that the distribution has been proper, and all the creditors have been paid, the accounting procedure may not be necessary. If all parties involved including distributees and creditors sign waivers of their rights to object, the accounting will be approved by the Court without the necessity of a hearing. In small estates, it is even possible to dispense with an accounting altogether by having the interested parties sign an agreement to that effect.

Chapter V

INTER VIVOS TRUSTS

1. ALTERNATIVES TO A WILL

Will probate and the administration of an estate can be costly and inefficient -- postponing unduly the distribution of assets to heirs and increasing the expenses of managing the estate prior to distribution. While the use of trusts has traditionally been thought of as a tax-oriented method of disposition of assets for persons with substantial estates, the fact is that the trust, in the same way as is true of the will, may be a necessity for the person of moderate circumstances.

Persons looking to limit problems with their possessions after death will frequently create relationships during their lifetimes that enable a named party simply to take possession at death by the nature of the relationship itself or by an instrument other than a will. Thus, a life insurance policy will be applied for and owned by a wife, and even though the husband may pay the premiums, at his death, the wife will be entitled to the proceeds in accordance with the terms of the insurance policy and will not have to wait for the probate of her husband's will. Moreover, since she has been the owner of the policy, the proceeds are not part of her husband's estate.

But if the wife dies before her husband, under circumstances where the contingent beneficiary is not clearly provided for, the policy may revert to the husband's estate and create the very problems that were initially sought to be avoided. An insurance trust, however, operates to render all beneficiaries secure, to enable dispositions that are more flexible than the options provided by life insurance policies, and to create a viable machinery, other than a will, for the administration and distribution of death proceeds.

Insured pension plans operate on this basis. The trustees of the pension plan are actually the owners of the life insurance policies issued on participants. So long as a participant designates other than his estate as the beneficiary, the proceeds of the policy will be paid at his death to the named beneficiary or beneficiaries, and the proceeds will not be included in the gross estate of the participant.

2. JOINT OWNERSHIP

Many husbands and wives will hold property jointly -- as the phrase goes, "joint tenants with right of survivorship (JTWROS)." While, on the death of either one, the surviving spouse immediately becomes the sole owner, the joint tenancy can create more problems than it answers. First of all, since joint tenancies are frequently created in later years, when a husband wants to assure that his wife will have immediate and continuing access to bank accounts, interest, securities and the dividends on securities, i.e., all liquid assets, there is always the danger that the way it is done will create gift tax liability -- but without corresponding estate tax benefits (although gift taxes do constitute a deductible item against calculated estate tax). For, Internal Revenue Service will assume in a joint tenancy that the assets were the property of the deceased and, therefore, totally includable in his estate. This can be disproved, but the burden is on the survivor, not on the I.R.S. And if the transfer was made within three years of the deceased's death, I.R.S. will assume a gift in contemplation of death and will likewise cast the assets into the estate of the deceased. So, while the wife gains immediate and continuing access to all such "joint" property, she may inherit, as well, a needless estate tax problem. This can be a particularly bitter pill when it was she and not her husband who was the source of the asset in question. If she can't establish proof to overcome the presumption that it was her husband's, it is treated as part of his estate, regardless of the facts. Frequently, for example, savings bank accounts held jointly actually reflect the wife's savings from household monies. But how does one convince I.R.S. of that?

A more sophisticated approach, and one that is created by law in so-called "community property" states, is the "tenancy in common." Under tenancy in common, each of the holders is deemed to own an undivided or unspecified half of the asset so held. While this assures that the survivor's half is indeed hers, she does not automatically inherit her husband's half, which then will face probate, estate taxes, etc. It is half a loaf, and therefore, at least half unsatisfactory.

3. USING INTER VIVOS TRUSTS

Thus, the trust emerges as the method for accomplishing

the objectives, each gift to the trust being clearly identified as to its source. At the death of either party, then, the other has complete continuity in the control and administration of the assets, even to the extent that what will happen at the death of the survivor has been planned and provided for.

Take, for example, a couple in later years who have amassed a modest estate. (Remember that an estate of $120,000, while no small figure, if properly arranged, can pass free of estate taxes. The marital deduction would account for $60,000 and the personal exemption would cover the remaining $60,000.) But such assets, if not properly structured, could leave the surviving spouse with endless administrative and mechanical problems -- will probate, retaining an attorney, assets to be transferred on company records, etc. -- all problems that a spouse is least well equipped to face at the death of the mate.

Suppose, this couple wants to enjoy for their lifetime complete dominion over the assets, including the income, but wants to assure that children will take at death of the survivor, with no problems of administration. A trust can be set up for the children. Since the couple may not be concerned either with income tax currently or with estate taxes ultimately, they can convey to themselves as trustees for the ultimate benefit of their named children, equally share and share alike. At the death of one of them, only those assets identified as part of that person's estate would be so charged. Even if all the assets are so identified and charged, the estate tax is currently disposed of; the survivor enjoys thereafter only the income for the rest of his or her life; and the children take title automatically at the survivor's death. No probate, no administrative expenses, no problems.

To accomplish totally the desired results, the couple may want to create different trusts, some revocable and some irrevocable, as is more fully described below. Thus, in the illustration above, the children may be named as trustees and the gifts made to the trust irrevocably. The life income is provided for the husband and wife. Gift taxes, if any, are paid currently; income tax is paid by the income beneficiaries as they receive it; and if all incidents of their ownership have been renounced, there may be no estate tax chargeable. (The rules governing these situations and the doctrine of "attribution" in family transactions are very technical in terms of defining estate tax liability. Hence, the implicit caveat that estate taxes may or may not be chargeable in this type of situation).

To apply these concepts specifically, let us take a husband who, early in his family life, sits down with his attorney and makes a will. Through the years, as circumstances change, he will amend that will either by codicils to the original, or by revoking the original will and creating a new one. Let us assume, however, that conscious of these problems, he has come down to his later years with precisely the will that suits his needs. He has taken that portion of his assets that qualify for marital deduction and bequeathed them to his wife. She will take these assets free of estate tax. Let us say he has also created a trust of all the remaining assets. This would be a testamentary trust since it is created under his will. By leaving the income therefrom to his wife, with power to invade the trust assets for her benefit, he actually gives her the control of the assets in the trust, but through the vehicle of the trust, at her death, these assets will pass to his children without liability for estate tax. If his estate is $120,000, and assuming all the assets remain intact, there will be no tax on his estate (the combination of the marital deduction and the personal exemption). And, when his wife dies, the trust assets will pass to the children outside the wife's estate, and her personal exemption will cover that portion that she had taken by the marital deduction, and now passes to her children. Again, no tax. What, then, is wrong with this method? Only the delays, travail and expense of will probate and estate administration.

The fact is that the precise result can be accomplished inter vivos (i.e., doing the same things while one is alive). Thus, let us say that, as to half the assets, they are placed in a revocable trust -- Sam Jones and Elsie Jones in trust for Myron Jones and Sylvia Jones (their children). Since by definition, the trust is revocable, they part with no control of the assets. If Sam dies, Elsie continues as the trustee of the revocable trust. But when Elsie dies, the children automatically take ownership, and they need not wait for probate of a will and distribution by an executor. Their ownership is immediate and automatic. These assets will be part of Sam's estate, but since Elsie continues as trustee of this revocable trust, she in fact takes as a surviving spouse. If the assets have been planned within an arithmetic calculation of total estate, there should be no estate tax on Elsie's taking these assets. When they pass to the children at Elsie's death, her personal exemption of $60,000 will be credited against these assets for purposes of determining tax on her estate.

Now, as to the second half of the estate, Sam and Elsie

create in their lifetimes, an irrevocable trust, naming Myron and Sylvia as the trustees. Sam and Elsie retain income for their lives. This is deemed an "incident or ownership" and will cast these assets into Sam's estate. At his death, estate tax, after taking credit for his personal exemption of $60,000, will be due on these assets. But even though Elsie continues to get the income, the assets of this irrevocable trust are not part of her estate. At her death, they are not includable in her estate, but pass to the designated beneficiaries free of estate tax.

Thus, the combination of revocable and irrevocable trusts, set up during a lifetime, accomplish the same results as a well-drawn marital deduction will, but the problems of probate, administrative expense, delay, etc., are totally eliminated. As to gift tax, it should be noted that a husband and wife are entitled to a lifetime exemption of $60,000, plus $6,000 free of tax to all entities or persons to whom they might make such a gift in a given year. Thus, in the year that an irrevocable trust is set up, assuming two trusts for each of two children, $72,000 of assets may be gifted without incurring gift tax liability. Thereafter, each year the couple may give to each trust an additional $6,000 in assets. Thus, on a continuing basis, the irrevocable trust becomes an ideal way of putting assets beyond the reach of probate and estate administration, though, since income is reserved, not necessarily a way of avoiding estate tax.

While the foregoing is based on the relatively simple situation of an estate of $120,000 consisting essentially of liquid assets -- bank accounts, stocks, bonds, etc., the program can likewise be extended to include the stock of close corporation businesses, real estate, or other types of assets that are best described as "illiquid."

To comprehend in depth how a program similar to that suggested here can be worked up, the material that follows deals in detail with revocable and irrevocable trusts and the language and mechanics of setting them up.

4. THE REVOCABLE TRUST

The previous chapter has dealt with inter vivos trusts, i.e., trusts that are created during the lifetime of the settlor (the person or persons creating the trust), as distinguished from testamentary trusts, which are those created by a Will.

An inter vivos trust takes effect while the settlor is still living; a testamentary trust takes effect at his death. The inter vivos trust may be said to lie somewhere between an outright gift and retention of property until it passed under a Will at the death of the property's owner. Inter vivos trusts, as we have seen, may be either revocable or irrevocable, and we have reviewed a program whereby the two may be combined to create, in effect, a currently operating testamentary disposition, without a Will.

The revocable trust, as its name implies, is one which the settlor can revoke at any time. Thus, it is not the giving away of anything, but rather a device to provide both efficient management of property with retaining ownership control. In terms of providing for after death, it sets up an arrangement under which the property that is put in the trust passes automatically to the beneficiary at death. Thus, the property is removed from probate and the ultimate heirs do not have to wait for an estate wind-up and distribution before taking over the assets.

A very simple revocable trust can be a savings bank account, in which the monies on deposit are held by the owner in trust for the ultimate beneficiary. At the owner's death, the beneficiary becomes the owner of the account. Thus, in our illustration in the previous chapter, our hypothetical Jones couple could create a bank account

> SAM & ELSIE JONES
> itf (in trust for)
> MYRON JONES and SYLVIA JONES

Sam and Elsie have the right to deposit and to withdraw. They have the right to the interest. They have the right to close the account if they so choose. They have the right to alter the beneficiaries. And, in the event of Sam's death, Elsie will continue to enjoy the same rights of absolute control, and at her death, the account will pass to Myron and Sylvia. Thus, two successive transfers are assured, without any further instrument or ultimate administration.

As in joint tenancy, estate tax implications are the same. If Sam dies first, unless Elsie can affirmatively prove that all or a portion of the assets were hers, the bank account will be includable in Sam's gross estate for tax purposes. But it will be one of the assets that is entitled to pass to Elsie under the marital deduction. At Elsie's death, it will be includable in her gross estate. But in neither case has a Will provision been necessary to make the disposition of the property. The ownership having been retained, there is at no time a gift tax liability.

Stocks and bonds can likewise be held in a revocable trust. So long as the registrar of a company's stock is advised in writing, certificates will be issued in precisely the manner requested by the owner. As with the bank account, securities will then pass by the designation on the certificates. In our illustration, after both Sam and Elsie are gone, Myron and Sylvia would own stocks and bonds outright that had been set up in revocable trusts. (Note the caveat, however, discussed further on, that it may be advisable to name Myron or Elsie or both as trustees of the revocable trust to avoid any implication that what has been attempted is a testamentary disposition without the required mechanics of the State's Statute of Wills.)

Even the stock of a closely held family corporation can be dealt with more flexibly through the revocable trust than through a testamentary provision in a Will. Earlier, in dealing with the marital deduction, it was said that a marital deduction trust could be used in a Will to give stock to a wife in trust, while having the son, as trustee, run the business and make the decisions. Under the revocable trust, the owner of the business can actually have a test run of his son's ability to manage.

Let us assume, for example, that Sam wants his business to pass to Myron at his death. But he does not want to name Myron as the executor under his Will. If he bequeathes the stock in his company to Myron under his Will or to Myron as a trustee for Elsie under the Will, Myron will not actually have the ownership, either outright or as a trustee, until the Will is probated and distribution is made. Perhaps, Elsie or Sylvia, feeling that Myron should not have the business, decides to contest the Will. There follows a lengthy litigation in which the ownership of the business is thrown into uncertainty -- probably, with dangerous implications for the business's future.

Or, perhaps, under the typically broad mandate given an executor under a Will, the executor decides to sell the business. Myron may have no business (although he would be entitled to the proceeds of the sale) and Sam's desire and intent for Myron and for the business will have been thwarted.

On the other hand, a revocable trust, perhaps with Sam himself as trustee, and Myron as beneficiary, leaves no room for doubt and assures continuity. For, at Sam's death the business passes automatically to Myron. Or, if he desires to divide his stock between his wife and children, he can appoint Myron as trustee with him. At his death, Myron would administer the business for the benefit of himself, his mother, and his sister. This also affords Sam a chance to test Myron's management ability. But since, while he is alive, Sam remains in control, if Myron should become difficult, Sam can "fire" him as trustee and remake his arrangements. The point is that the revocable trust enables Sam to retain control while assuring that, at his death, what he wants to accomplish will happen automatically.

This focuses on one of the prime advantages of the revocable trust as a method of estate planning. While the owner-settlor lives, he puts into operation under management he selects, a program that will protect his family and assure the carrying out of his wishes after his death. He is able, while he is still alive to have a preview of how his estate plan would operate. Since he retains the power to amend or remake the trust, he can make necessary changes before his death -- and much more easily than by remaking a Will.

So far, we have looked at the revocable inter vivos trust essentially as a "testamentary" disposition, as a substitute for a bequest proviso in a Will. But it serves other purposes as well. Suppose, for example, that Sam and Elsie want to maintain control and ownership of property, but want to shift the income from that property to Myron and Sylvia, who may be in a lower tax bracket. If they held a joint tenancy bank account, interest earned would be chargeable to them, even if they gave it to the children. They would have to report it for tax purposes. Likewise, the dividends on stocks and the interest on bonds would be chargeable to Sam and Elsie, even if they gave them to the children. But if these income-producing items are held in revocable trust, the income may be paid or shifted to the beneficiaries, or income may be allocated as best suits the needs of settlors and beneficiaries alike.

Then, too, a revocable trust may be set up under which someone else will manage the property. Let us assume that Sam and Elsie would prefer to have Myron handle the stocks and bonds portfolio, but without giving up either ownership or income. The trust arrangement will then designate,

MYRON JONES
itf SAM AND ELSIE JONES

with a provision that, at their death, the assets will pass to Myron and Sylvia Jones, equally, share and share alike.

We revert to the caveat mentioned above in the use of revocable trusts. Since, by nature, it is a testamentary disposition accomplished inter vivos, without a Will, the question may arise whether the retained powers are not so great as to make the trust instrument fall within the requirements of a Statute of Wills. Over the last three decades, the trend of the courts has been away from strict interpretation, but the problem does underscore the need for an attorney with whom one can review plans. For, a revocable trust that would be held to be subject to the Statute of Wills would be void, resulting in totally defeating the settlor's intent and throwing the estate into a total muddle.

By way of summarizing the advantages of the revocable trust, it should not be viewed simply in the context of an alternative to an irrevocable trust (which we shall next examine). It has its own place in an estate plan and is more an alternative to a Will. Among the advantages are the following:

1) It affords the settlor control and flexibility -- a workable substitute for a Will.

2) It avoids the expenses of probate and the corresponding fees of executors, attorneys and appraisers -- usually based on the size of the probate estate. Whatever can be removed from probate means less expense.

3) The domicile of the trust can be different from that of the settlor. This is a valuable option in terms of selecting a domicile for assets that best meets the settlor's tax objectives, as well as convenience of administration.

4) It avoids property being tied up in probate during which time it is not available to heirs.

5) It minimizes the disruptive effect of the death of a settlor on his business. Court supervision is avoided, and the business can be continued by the person intended to manage it.

6) It is a device for the management of property by persons whose competence is trusted and, at least, can be tested.

5. THE IRREVOCABLE TRUST

As a revocable trust is comparable to bequests made under a Will, an irrevocable trust is comparable to an outright gift. The irrevocable trust, by definition, cannot be revoked by the settlor. They are gifts in trust. But they do offer more flexibility than the outright gift. Thus, the management of the trust may be lodged in someone other than the beneficiary. It is even possible for the settlor himself to retain these powers, but careful consideration must be given to the tax consequences of such retained powers.

The degree of the beneficiary's interest may be specifically defined. His right to the corpus of the trust may be deferred or otherwise circumscribed. Spendthrift clauses may protect the income from creditors. Where minors are involved, the inconvenience of guardianship arrangements is avoided. Perhaps, most important, the trust can provide for lifetime beneficiaries as well as ultimate beneficiaries. This cannot be accomplished by outright gift.

Compared to the revocable trust, there are additional advantages to the irrevocable trust as a tool in estate planning. In fact, judiciously used along with the revocable trust, the results of a sophisticated marital deduction Will can be achieved without the need for the Will and its attendant probate and estate administration disadvantages.

The tax benefits can be at least as extensive and even more flexible than with the outright gift. For, where no incidents of ownership are retained by the settlor, he retains no right to income and no control over property in trust; that property is not includable in his estate. For the wealthy, the taxable estate can be substantially reduced, yet without simply giving away assets to heirs who may not yet be mature enough to handle them.

But what of the person in more moderate circumstances who may create financial problems for himself during his lifetime by giving assets away irrevocably -- even in trust. Even for him there are advantageous tax consequences tailored to his particular situation. Thus, let us assume a gift in trust made irrevocably, but reserving the income therefrom for the settlor's life and for the life of his wife thereafter. (The illustration of Sam and Elsie Jones.) The likelihood is that the assets will be deemed includable in the settlor's gross estate. (If he has paid gift taxes, there will be a credit for them against estate taxes that may be due). But what is achieved is that just as with a testamentary trust under a Will, the survivor's wife is just a lifetime beneficiary and at her decease, the assets pass to the ultimate beneficiaries outside her estate. So even though the trust property may be includable in the settlor's gross estate, it bypasses the wife's estate. And again, the entire process takes place outside probate and estate administration.

These consequences would be neither worse nor better if the settlor made himself the trustee. But it is advisable that the successor trustee after his death be someone other than the wife.

Or the wife, if originally a joint trustee with her husband, would be well advised to resign in favor of another trustee, perhaps one of the beneficiaries. For the whole objective is to avoid any situation in which the assets could be cast back into the wife's estate. Her merely receiving the income from the trust would not create such a risk. But any exercise of dominion or power over the trust property might do so. One useful approach to the problem of continuing trusteeship is to name a bank. But there is a charge for the service.

As pointed out earlier, the combination of revocable and irrevocable trusts can be used for an estate of not more than $120,000 in such a way as to leave no estate tax liability on the settlor's death, and likewise no estate tax liability on the wife's death. As the size of the estate increases, the combination can nevertheless result in minimizing taxes on the settlor's estate, and likewise on the portion of the estate that ultimately passes from the surviving spouse to the children.

In general, discussion has been from the vantage point of the person of comfortable but moderate circumstances, leaving a modest estate which it is to his advantage to control until his death. But for the person who will leave a more substantial estate, some of the dos and donts, together with their taxable consequences, may be helpful. Here, the objective may be to move income over to a lower-taxed person or entity, and to avoid inclusion of the trust assets in the gross estate. Since this almanac is not designed as a tax or estate planning manual, observations will be brief. The interested reader is best referred to his own attorney for details.

For the person who wants to assure that all tax consequences of a gift of property in trust will fall elsewhere, the gift should be made with no strings attached.

1) Do not reserve income. The income will be taxed to you, and most likely, the property itself will be deemed includable in your estate.

2) Do not reserve any incidents of ownership in the property. Even a contingent reversion of the property to you will make it includable in your estate.

3) Do not reserve any right to change beneficiaries or alter the terms under which their interests vest.

4) Do not retain any power of management or administration over the trust assets. In fact, appoint someone other than yourself or your wife as trustee. (Her appointment might be "attributed" to you as yours would be to her.)

5) Make up your mind that you are giving property away --
in trust, rather than outright, so that there can be a measure of
built-in control. But the administration and supervision of that
control must be in someone else. You can lay down the game plan,
but you can't play in the game!

As has been the consistent emphasis in this discussion on
the use of trusts, they do offer tools of estate planning that can
achieve more flexibly and easily than a Will the desired results.
Certainly, they can operate to place the Will in perspective -- an
instrument to tie down anything you may miss. But the inter vivos
trusts should be focal in effective planning.

Too often people try to make moves designed to protect each
other and their children a "do-it-yourself" affair. This can create
incredible problems. Thus, the matters suggested here must be
referred to an attorney for proper planning, drafting and execution. There will be a cost, but such service now will be a fraction
of what would be the cost later on, when attorneys must cope with
mistakes that have been made. One final word. Devices such as
trusts are not useful exclusively for the wealthy, but are part of
everyone's planning for the disposition of his property at his
death.

6.   FORM OF IRREVOCABLE TRUST

The following is a simple irrevocable trust, suitable to the
illustration of Sam and Elsie Jones

"This declaration of trust is made the ... day of ....,
19..., between SAM JONES and ELSIE JONES, his wife, hereinafter called Settlors, and MYRON JONES of New York City, hereinafter called Trustee, in order to establish a trust for the purposes and under the terms and conditions hereafter stated.

The Settlors give, grant, convey and assign to the trustee
the following property:

(here specify the property transferred)

The Trustee acknowledges delivery of said property and
agrees to hold and manage it, together with any property added
to it and becoming a part of the trust estate, in trust for the uses
and in the manner herein set forth.

1. The trustee shall pay net income derived from the trust estate to Sam and Elsie Jones, as long as they shall live, and upon the death of one, thereafter to the other. (Note that this reservation of income will throw the trust assets into Sam's estate, if he predeceases Elsie. To remove the trust property from the estate of either, the income beneficiary should be other than Sam or Elsie. If Sam alone were the settlor, it would still be questionable, under the rules of attribution, whether Sam could avoid the property being includable in his estate.)

2. Upon the death of the survivor of Sam and Elsie Jones, the Trustee shall divide the trust property into equal shares and shall forthwith distribute one such share to Sylvia Jones and one such share to Myron Jones, and upon that event, the Trust shall terminate.

3. This trust is entered into in the State of New York and shall be interpreted and controlled by the laws of that State. (Note: Sam and Elsie may be domiciled in Florida, but they have the right to set up the trust in New York, where Myron is domiciled, and the trust property will follow Myron and not Sam and Elsie. It happens that Florida has a tax on intangibles, although it does not have a state income tax. So, deciding the domicile of the trust involves weighing tax factors pro and con.)

Unlike a Will, a trust instrument requires nothing more than the ordinary contractual agreement, i.e., signatures of the settlors and the trustee. Notarization of signatures is frequently useful, so that proof of execution of the instrument, if ever required, can be furnished by an objective outsider. But the witnesses required to the signing of a Will are not necessary to the execution of a trust instrument.

The foregoing instrument can be enlarged upon. For example, if Sam is the settlor, and he creates life income for Elsie, he can also include a provision for invasion of the trust corpus for the benefit of Elsie. This puts the instrument on all fours with the testamentary trust in a Will. And just as can be accomplished in a Will, a settlor may provide for grandchildren, for contingencies in the event of the death of an ultimate beneficiary, etc.

7. POWERS OF TRUSTEES

Whether under a testamentary trust set up in a Will or an inter vivos irrevocable trust, it is usual to include broadly defined powers of the trustees. Typical provision is the following:

"The Trustee shall have the following powers with respect to any and all property held by him, as Trustee:

1. To sell such property at public or private sale, without court approval, and to lease the same even for a term which may continue beyond the intended duration of the trust. Such lease may be given with or without option to purchase.

2. To exchange or abandon such property.

3. To borrow money with or without security and to repay any such borrowings from principal and income in such manner and in such proportions as the Trustee determines.

4. To manage, maintain, improve, subdivide, and otherwise exploit and develop by any means all real and personal property in the trust; to enter into contracts and grant options with respect thereto, and to retain such property intact throughout the life of this trust.

5. To retain stocks, securities and mortgages and other intangible assets in the trust, and to invest and reinvest and otherwise deal with such assets without respect to laws concerning the investment of trust funds, to vote stock and securities in his name, or in the name of his nominees; to exercise conversion and subscription rights and pay such sums as may be appropriate with respect thereto; to grant options with respect to all such property; to lease such property for purposes of producing oil and gas, and to participate in the recapitalization, reorganization, consolidation or merger of any company or companies whose stock or other securities are held in the trust funds in such manner and to such extent as he may deem advisable and to share in the expenses thereof.

6. To collect and receive all dividends, interest, rent and other income owing to the trust.

7. To maintain, continue to operate, or terminate in any manner or at any time any commercial enterprise forming a part of the trust estate.

8. To employ and pay counsel or agents for any purpose including the making of investments.

100

9. To compromise or otherwise settle all claims by or against the trust estate.

10. Where the trustee is required to divide property passing under this declaration of trust, he need not physically divide or segregate such property, but may retain it intact and apportion undivided interests therein to the shares of beneficiaries entitled thereto.

11. To exercise full rights, powers and dominion over the property, the same as an owner thereof. The generality of this power shall not be limited by the specific references of the preceding clauses of this provision.

12. None of the foregoing powers are to be interpreted in derogation of any right of the trustee under the law.

13. The foregoing shall be undertaken to the extent and under such terms and conditions as the trustee shall in his judgment deem advisable and proper, exercising the discretion that a prudent man would use in the management of property held for the benefit of others. The judgment of the Trustee with respect to the diversification of assets shall be final."

Needless to say, these are broad powers, rendering the choice of trustee, whether under a Will or an inter vivos trust a matter of serious consideration and great selectivity.

Chapter VI

NOTE ON THE TAX REFORM ACT OF 1976

The Tax Reform Act of 1976 made sweeping changes in the estate and gift tax provisions of the Internal Revenue Code. These are the first major revisions in these fields in 28 years. Most of the law has been essentially unchanged since the twenties.

This new tax law makes changes which makes it compelling that every will, revocable trust, and buy-sell agreement be reviewed. In many cases, estate plan revisions of one kind or another will be of great importance. Readers who presently hold estate programs should certainly contact their attorneys for a review.

Nor is the change all bad! For estates whose gross value is $350,000 and less, most of the news is very good indeed. Their potential transfer taxes have been substantially reduced. Skillful planning together with your attorney may result in exempting combined husband and wife estates of $250,000 to over $400,000 from federal estate tax. Individual estates grossing less than $120,000 will virtually all pass to beneficiaries without any federal estate tax, and comparatively little change will be necessary to achieve this end.

While no attempt will be made here to detail the changes brought about by this landmark tax legislation, it might prove helpful to the reader for us to describe the unification of estate and gift taxes provision both as a dramatic example of a major change which will, hopefully, influence our readers to communicate with their attorneys in connection with their estate planning programs, both existing and contemplated.

Although the federal estate and gift tax laws have always been loosely interrelated, until now they have constituted two separate, essentially independent taxes. The federal gift tax rates were substantially lower than the federal estate tax rates; lifetime gifts — unless made within three years of death and held to have been in contemplation of death — would remove the amount of the gift from taxation at the donor's highest estate tax brackets and reallocate it to the bottom of the gift tax rate schedule.

Effective January 1, 1977, the separate estate and gift tax schedules were combined into a single, new, transfer tax, as indicated in the Table.

As this transfer tax is a *unified* gift and estate tax, the cumulative amount of post-1976 taxable gifts is added to the value of the taxable estate in determining the amount of the estate tax.

Under the new law, with its add-back inclusion for estate tax purposes of taxable gifts given away, the principal remaining *tax* benefit to be achieved by life-time giving will be the removal from taxation at the donor's highest estate tax brackets of all postgift increases in the value of assets given away, whether due to growth or inflation, as well as the income from these assets and any gift tax paid on the gifts, provided the donor survives the gift by three years. An additional benefit is that the income from the transferred assets may be subject to lower income taxes if the donee is in a lower income tax than the donor.

Finally, henceforth gifts coming within the $3,000 annual gift tax exclusion per donee will be much more important. These gifts will *not* be included in computing one's estate tax, even if made on one's deathbed. Thus, in many situations, these $3,000 gifts should be made to each child and grandchild, and perhaps his spouse, as soon as conveniently possible each year, normally in January.

But, again, we urge the reader to turn to his own attorney for much more of the same in connection with the changes and benefits of the Tax Reform Act.

CHART No. 4
New Transfer Tax Rates

Taxable Amount (Base)	Base Tax	Tax Rate on Excess
Under 10,000		18% of total transfer
10,000	1,800	20%
20,000	3,800	22%
40,000	8,200	24%
60,000	13,000	26%
80,000	18,200	28%
100,000	23,800	30%
150,000	38,800	32%
250,000	70,800	34%
500,000	155,800	37%
750,000	248,300	39%
1,000,000	345,800	41%
1,250,000	448,300	43%
1,500,000	555,800	45%
2,000,000	780,800	49%
2,500,000	1,025,800	53%
3,000,000	1,290,800	57%
3,500,000	1,575,800	61%
4,000,000	1,880,800	65%
4,500,000	2,205,800	69%
5,000,000	2,550,800	70%

Chapter VII

THE "LIVING" WILL

A living will is not a legally binding document in most states. It is the written declaration of a wish not to be treated for a terminal illness. Frequently it is characterized as the "pull the plug" will.

The purpose of a living will is to give a person the right to determine the nature of his/her death. The *N. Y. Times* reported in December, 1984, that a growing segment of the population "has had a terrifying experience, themselves or a loved one losing their rights, to medical technology." As a result there is an increasing amount of pressure on the state legislatures to legalize the individual's right to advance directions regarding the stopping of life-sustaining procedures that would only "prolong artificially the dying process." Where living wills are not formally recognized by legislation, doctors and judges often use such documents as indications of incompetent patients' wishes.

It is a recognized document, included in a widely used legal forms book, *Modern Legal Forms* (*see* Living Will form at the end of this chapter). But the Living Will has not yet been tested in the courts. It is, however, enforceable to the extent that should a legal, medical, or ethical question arise concerning treatment, the patient's wishes are formally stated in writing. As such, there can be no question that the signer has decided to exercise the right to refuse treatment.

There are two important steps that a person can take to insure that his/her Living Will is enforced. First, it should be promptly discussed with the doctor involved.

The doctor should agree with the patient's decision to sign the document, or at least be willing to honor the patient's request regardless of personal sentiments. If such an agreement cannot be reached, there will be great problems in enforcing the Living Will. In this kind of situation the patient might seek out another doctor who is sympathetic to this situation. A second step is to discuss it with family members, making certain that they take over the responsibility of consulting with the doctor if the patient becomes unable to do so personally.

In some states it is possible to execute a Power of Attorney, appointing a specific individual to make decisions in one place.

The Living Will should be witnessed by two adults. This is done as proof of execution, to establish that the individual did in fact sign, and did so of his/her own free will. It is probably a good idea to have it notarized as further proof of the seriousness of one's intent.

There is no clear answer to the question of how long the Living Will remains effective. Since, however, the more recent the date the more likely that a court would accept it as the expression of the patient's wishes when he/she was last competent, the patient should periodically (at least once a year) redate the Living Will. The new date should be initialled to make clear that his/her wishes are unchanged.

Copies of the Living Will should be very accessible, not placed in a safe deposit box or otherwise filed away where it might not be found until it is too late. Most people give copies to their doctors and next of kin as well as to religious advisors, lawyers, or friend - or anyone else who might be in a position to be making decisions about the patient's treatment.

More complete information about the Living Will can be obtained from an organization called:

Concern for Dying
250 West 57th Street
New York, New York 10107

The information in this chapter was drawn from that source.*

---

*To My Family, My Physician, My Lawyer
and All Others Whom It May Concern*

Death is as much a reality as birth, growth, maturity and old age — it is the one certainty of life. If the time comes when I can no longer take part in decisions for my own future, let this statement stand as an expression of my wishes and directions, while I am still of sound mind.

If at such a time the situation should arise in which there is no reasonable expectation of my recovery from extreme physical or mental disability, I direct that I be allowed to die and not be kept alive by medications, artificial means or "heroic measures". I do, however, ask that medication be mercifully administered to me to alleviate suffering even though this may shorten my remaining life.

This statement is made after careful consideration and is in accordance with my strong convictions and beliefs. I want the wishes and directions here expressed carried out to the extent permitted by law. Insofar as they are not legally enforceable, I hope that those to whom this Will is addressed will regard themselves as morally bound by these provisions.

Signed _____

Date _____

Witness _____

Witness _____

Copies of this request have been given to _____

_____

_____

_____

---

* This Living Will is reprinted with permission of this organization.

STATES HAVING "NATURAL DEATH" OR "RIGHT TO DIE LEGISLATION"*

"Living Will" Legislation, also known as "Natural Death" or "Right-to-Die" Acts.

State	Became law	Time after which directive must be reexecuted	Form provided	Hospital and physician legally protected unless negligent	Binding on physician	Can be executed by adult in good health	In order to be binding, must be re-executed after patient becomes terminal
Alabama (Act 772, S.30)	May 1981	None	Yes -	Yes	Yes, or physician must transfer patient to another physician	Yes	No
Arkansas (Act 879)	July 1977	None	No	Yes	Same as New Mexico	Yes	No
California (A.B 3060)	Jan. 1977	5 years	Yes	Yes	Yes, if directive signed 14 days after patient becomes terminal	Yes, but not binding unless patient is terminal	Yes
District of Columbia (4-68)	Feb. 1982	None	Yes	Yes	Yes	Yes	No, but physician must provide written certification and confirmation of terminal condition
Idaho (S.B. 1164)	July 1977	5 years	Yes	Yes	Same as New Mexico (if patient is terminal and cannot communicate)	Same as California	Yes
Kansas (S 99)	April 1979	None	Suggested form	Yes	Yes	Yes	No
Nevada (A.B. 8)	July 1977	None	Yes	Yes	No	Yes	No (but directive is not binding at any time)
New Mexico (S.B. 16)	June 1977	None	No	Yes, but physician must show "reasonable care and judgment"	Yes, but no penalty if physician does not comply	Yes	No
North Carolina (S.B. 504)	July 1977	None	Yes	Physicians are protected; hospitals not specifically protected	No	Yes	Same as Nevada
Oregon (S.B. 438)	June 1977	5 years	Yes	Yes	Same as California	Same as California	Yes
Texas (S.B. 148)	Aug. 1977	5 years	Yes	Yes	Same as California	Same as California	Yes
Vermont (Act 141)	April 1982	None	Yes, but document need not be in that form	Yes	Yes, if physician cannot comply, has duty to inform patient and family and/or transfer patient to physician who will	Yes	No
Washington (H 264)	March 1979	None	Suggested form	Yes	No	Yes	No

* Reprinted with permission of Concern for Dying, 250 West 57th Street, New York, New York 10107.

Chapter VIII

THE UNIFORM ANATOMICAL GIFT ACT

There has emerged in recent years an increasing amount of interest on the part of the public to donate all or any part of the human body for the use of medical science at the time of death. This use may be either for medical or dental education, research, advancement of medical or dental science, therapy or transplantation.

There were no laws dealing with organ donation before 1950. But medical science moved quickly ahead during the 1950's and 1960's when kidney transplants began to take place and then, in 1967, the remarkable event of the first human heart transplant. The legal issue then arose, could passing one vital organ from one body to another be legal?

The National Conference of the Commissioners on Uniform State Laws prepared the Uniform Anatomical Gift Act in subsequent years and by 1972 all fifty states had adopted the Act.

This legislation provides guidelines dealing with the rights and duties of donors and donees of anatomical gifts. It is possible for a person to make a gift of all or certain parts of his/her body and, subject to the terms of the gift, still have the usual embalming, funeral services, and custody of the body in the surviving spouse or next of kin.

In almost all of the fifty states any person at least 18 years of age who is of sound mind may make a gift of his/her body or any part thereof. Alaska provides for the age of 19 and Rhode Island requires that the person be 21.

In order of priority, the following persons may also give all or any part of the deceased person's body: the spouse; an adult son or daughter; either parent; an adult brother or sister; a guardian of the person deceased at the time of his/her death; another person authorized or under obligation to dispose of the body. However, if the deceased has indicated his/her objection to such a gift, the gift cannot be made by anyone under any circumstances. Furthermore, opposition by a member of the same class or a prior class of the priorities stated here prevents the gift.

While most states agree with the foregoing, in Florida an adult son or daughter can veto the gift. Rhode Island and California have laws that provide that the relatives of the deceased cannot make a donation in violation of the deceased's religious conviction.

The gift may be made immediately after death or even before death. For the use of certain parts of the body and particularly for use in transplants, the gift must be made prior to the moment of death. The law recognizes this and permits such use.

The following are authorized by law to receive the gift of the body or any part thereof: (1) any hospital, surgeon or physician, for medical or dental education, research, advancement of medical or dental science, therapy or transplantation; (2) any accredited medical or dental institution for education, research, advancement of medical or dental science, or therapy; (3) any "bank" or storage facility for medical or dental education, research, advancement of medical or dental science, therapy or transplantation; (4) any specified individual for therapy or transplantation needed by him/her.

The gift need not specify to whom it is to be given. If the gift does specify to whom it is to be given and this is not convenient, another doctor or institution may accept the gift. Such doctor or institution has the right to either accept or reject the gift.

The law specifically provides that a gift of all or part of

112

the body may be made by a will. Such a gift is effective upon the death of the testator without waiting for probate. If the will is not probated, or if it is declared invalid for testamentary reasons, the gift, to the extent that it has been acted upon in good faith, remains valid and in effect.

A gift may also be made by a document other than a will. This document must, however, be signed by the person in the presence of at least two witnesses who must sign the document in his/her presence. It is not necessary for the document to be delivered during the person's lifetime to the doctor or medical institution. The gift becomes effective upon the death of the person.

The document may be a card designed to be carried on the person. Uniform cards for organ and tissue donation are available on request from doctors as well as from cooperating agencies as the National Kidney Foundation, New York City, and the Tissue Bank of the U.S. Naval Medical School, Bethesda, Maryland. These cards make it easy for a person to assure use of his/her organs or tissues after death for transplantation into patients with diseased hearts, kidneys, livers, eyes, etc.

In nearly all of the states a person's driver's license provides space to indicate a person's desire to donate all or part of his/her body.

If a donee such as a medical school accepts a gift of the entire body, the donee may authorize the embalming and burial of the remains. But if the gift is for transplantation, the obligation to dispose of the remains would fall upon the next of kin.

In order to carry out a donor's wishes, it is crucial that a determination of when he/she is dead is made. Most state laws provide that the time of death be certified by one or two physicians who are in attendance with the donor at the time of death. These doctors may not participate in the removal or transplantation of the organ.

A number of states have modified the uniform law in order to accomplish the objective of carying out the desired transplant. For example, a few states permit coroners to remove tissue during an autopsy. Other states provide that funeral directors or certain other technicians can do similar types of removals and transplants.

The Uniform Anatomical Gift Act does not cover the question of whether or not it will be permissible to buy or sell organs. Most statutes do not cover this question. Mississippi, however, permits a person over 18 to make a contract for the donation at his/her death. On the other hand, Delaware law forbids the sale of organs.*

* The Organ Donation Hotline has a toll free number: 800-24DONOR.

UNIFORM DONOR CARD

....
Print or type name of donor

In the hopes that I may help others, I hereby make this anatomical gift, if medically acceptable, to take effect upon my death. The words and marks below indicate my desires.

    I give (a).....any needed organs or parts

        (b).....only the following organs or parts

....
Specify the organs(s) or part(s)

fot the purpose of transplantation, therapy, medical research or education;

        (c).....my body for anatomical study if needed

Limitations or special wishes, if any:........................

Signed by the donor and the following two witnesses in the presence of each other:

....
Signature of Donor   Date of Birth of Donor

....
Date signed   City and State

....
Witness   Witness

This is a legal document under the Uniform Gift Act or similar laws.

Chapter IX

SURVEY OF THE ORIGIN AND
HISTORY OF WILLS

It is questionable whether instruments resembling a will, as we use the term today, were known to any early society except the Roman. Blackstone, the great English legal historian, wrote that in Rome wills were unknown before the laws of the Twelve Tables were compiled. Wills were allowed at Rome by the Twelve Tables, and they were executed with a great deal of ceremony before five citizens, the transaction taking the form of a purchase of the inheritance. Later, the praetors required seven witnesses who were required to place their seals and signatures to the instrument proving the transaction. Justinian's legislation provided for the signing by the testator and by witnesses and sealing by the witnesses.

For about three centuries preceding the Norman conquest the power of testamentary disposition was recognized and sanctioned in England. In the eighth century English law was familiar with an instrument executed in anticipation of death and by which the owner of property could have altered the course of intestate succession. The right to dispose of land and personal property by will was recognized by Anglo-Saxon folk law. The middle and lower classes seldom availed themselves of the right to make a will. But this does not necessarily mean that the right was confined to people of high rank, such as the king, bishops, and other nobles. It is probable that these were the only people who had enough property to be interested in the execution of a will.

Two important events took place in England that greatly affected the law of wills. Before the Norman Conquest there were no separate ecclesiastical courts in England. The Church and civil authorities were united both in administering the law as well as in making it. Under William I, the ecclesiastical courts were separated from the secular, resulting in a division of jurisdiction. The ecclesiastical courts acquired jurisdiction over intestate and testamentary succession to personal property, and the secular courts retained jurisdiction over succession to freehold estates, including jurisdiction over wills of real property. Important changes in the substantive law took place with respect to the two classes of wills.

Regardless of whether the feudal system existed in England before the arrival of the Normans, or was introduced by them, there is little doubt but that the system received its greatest development in England after their arrival. Feudalism had its influence in bringing about the abrogation of the right to devise land. Legal title to a freehold interest in land could pass only by a livery of seisin (a ceremonial delivery of land) or by proceedings in a court of record. Obviously a dead man (the testator) could not make such a livery of seisin, and the devisee, when the time came to enter, was confronted by the heir, from whom he had to obtain livery of seisin, the result probably being a refusal. A second factor was the lord's interest in the estate of his deceased tenant. The lord's right of escheat and wardship were subject to being defeated by a will. As long as feudal considerations controlled the law, the interests of the lord in the estate of his deceased tenant were protected against this possibility.

The development of the doctrine of primogeniture (the first-born's exclusive right to inheritance) was another factor that contributed to the abrogation of the right to devise land. The king's courts were interested in protecting the interest of the eldest son against any possible infringement by the making of a devise, from a military and political standpoint. These factors contributed to the disappearance of the right to devise land by the thirteenth century, except in a few localities where the jurisdiction of the king's justices did not extend. The borough courts in the cities had jurisdiction over burgage tenures, and the right to devise land was still recognized in these localities.

The restraint upon the power of devising land not surprisingly gave way to the demands of family affection and the desire for complete or independent dominion over land. The development of the doctrine of primogeniture and the later desire of the father to make some provision for his younger children was a compelling factor in the demand for a revival of the right to devise land. Landowners discovered that with the aid of the clerics, who controlled the court of chancery, they could dispose of their lands by will. They did so by means of the use (a trust in real estate). The way of doing this was to make a feoffment (a gift of a freehold accompanied by a livery of seisin), to hold the legal title to the use of the last will of the feoffor, and the latter could then devise the use, which devise was sustained in equity as an appointment by will. The feoffee was regarded as trustee for the person designated by the last will of the feoffor. The court of chancery supported the devise of the use as a disposition binding in conscience. The use was not subject to the feudal rules governing estates in land. This practice continued in England about a century, until the use became, by the *Statute of Uses* (1535), the legal estate. The *Statute of Uses* again destroyed the right of devising lands; but the disability was removed five years later by the *Statute of Wills* (1540).

In any case, before the enactment of the *Statute of Wills* in England the power of testamentary disposition of personal property was limited, unless the testator had no wife nor children. Whether this restriction was the early common law in England or a custom that existed only in some countries, it was recognized in the reign of Henry II as the doctrine of "reasonable parts" and, according to Glanville, as a part of the common law. According to this doctrine, if the testator had both wife and children he could dispose of only one-third of his personal property by will, while the other two-thirds was regarded as the reasonable share of the wife and children respectively. If he did not have a wife or children, but not both, he could dispose of one-half, the remainder belonging to the wife or children, as the case might have been. This restriction gradually disappeared. It was removed in a number of provinces by a series of statutes. The *Wills Act* (1837) in England extended the power to dispose of all of one's property, real or personal, which one was entitled to, either at law or in equity, at the time of one's death, by will.

The *Statute of Uses* had practically destroyed the right to devise lands in England. The demand for the right was so great that the *Statute of Wills* was passed, giving the right to devise all lands which were held in socage tenure and two-thirds of land held in knights' service. The right was given to "all and every person and persons," without any mention of age or sex. And the only specific requirement with regard to manner of execution was that the devise be in writing. About two years later Parliament passed a statute entitled "The Bill Concerning the Explanation of Wills" to explain and interpret the *Statute of Wills*. Wills made by married women, persons under twenty-one years of age, idiots, or insane persons were declared to be invalid by a provision of the latter statute. These two statutes sanctioned the power of devising lands only with respect to fee simple estates. Copyhold lands and estates *pur autre vie* remained undevisable. Both came within the description of real estate and so were not devisable at common law.

120

The only requirement of the *Statute of Wills* regarding the manner of execution of devises was that they should be in writing. The writing did not have to be made by the testator nor signed by him. Wills of personal property were not even required to be in writing to be valid. But it was customary to put them in writing, they were made before the testator's last illness. The opportunity for the perpetration of fraud was probably the compelling factor leading to the passage of the *Statute of Frauds* (1676). The fifth section of this Statute required devises not only to be in writing but signed by the testator, or by some person in his presence and by his express directions, and that they should be attested and subscribed in the presence of the testator by three or four credible witnesses.

The *Statute of Frauds* did not prohibit the making of verbal wills of personal property. But it did, however, subject them to strong restrictions in the manner of execution. Where the value of the estate bequeathed was more than thirty pounds the Statute required that the oral or nuncupative will had to be proved by oaths of at least three witnesses who were present at the making of the will. That they did bear witness that such was his will, and that such a will had to be made in the time of the last sickness of the testator in his home or where he had been resident for ten days or more before the making of the will. Also, the Statute provided that no testimony was admissible to prove an oral will (nuncupative will), unless the testimony had been reduced to writing within six months after the making of the will. Oral wills made by soldiers in military service or by mariners or seamen at sea were exempt from the provisions of this Statute.

The *Wills Act* established the same requirements for the execution for wills of realty and wills of personal property. It provided that *no* will (except those of soldiers in actual military service or mariners or seamen at sea) should be valid unless signed at the foot or end thereof by the testator, or by someone in his presence and by his direction. It further required that such signature was to be made or acknowledged by the testator in the presence of two or more witnesses present at the same time, and that such witnesses shall attest and subscribe the will in the presence of the testator. This Statute sanctions the power of disposing by will any realty or personal property to which the testator is entitled at the time of his death, and if it is not devised or bequeathed would devolve upon his heir (or heirs) at law or upon his executor.

The *Wills Act* is still in force in England, qualified by a provision that relaxes the rule concerning the position of the testator's signature at the foot or end of the will.

Some of the colonial assemblies in America enacted laws regulating the substantive law of wills which were based upon the English *Statute of Frauds*. In some of the colonies the provisions of this Statute were followed by usage. Legislation in the earlier states is based upon this Statute, while in those states which were admitted later into the Union regulate the law of wills based upon the *Wills Act*. There are statutes in every state regulating the substantive and procedural law of wills, and the two English statutes are models for most of the substantive law in this country.

The substantive law of wills in Louisiana is based upon the French civil law and New Mexico's law has a Spanish background.

Clearly, then, the origin and history of the law of wills in this country is essentially an English one and perhaps more than any other area of American law, it holds the greatest English orientation.

APPENDIX A
Court Titles Handling Probate of Wills

State	Court
Alabama	Probate Court
Alaska	Superior Court
Arizona	Superior Court
Arkansas	Probate Court
California	Superior Court
Colorado	District Court
Connecticut	Probate Court
Delaware	Court of Chancery
Florida	Circuit Court
Georgia	Probate Court
Hawaii	Circuit Court
Idaho	District Court (Magistrate Division)
Illinois	Circuit Court
Indiana	Probate Court
Iowa	District Court
Kansas	District Court
Kentucky	District Court
Louisiana	District Court
Maine	Probate Court
Maryland	Orphan's Court
Massachusetts	Probate & Family Court
Michigan	Probate Court
Minnesota	Probate Court
Mississippi	Chancery Court
Missouri	Circuit Court (Probate Division)
Montana	District Court
Nebraska	County Court
Nevada	District Court
New Hampshire	Probate Court
New Jersey	Surrogate's Court
New Mexico	Probate Court
New York	Surrogate's Court
North Carolina	Superior Court
North Dakota	County Court
Ohio	Court of Common Pleas (Probate Division)

Oklahoma	District Court
Oregon	Circuit Court
Pennsylvania	Orphan's Court
Rhode Island	Probate Court
South Carolina	Probate Court
South Dakota	Circuit Court
Tennessee	Probate Court
Texas	Probate Court
Utah	District Court
Vermont	Probate Court
Virginia	Circuit Court
Washington	Superior Court
West Virginia	County Commission
Wisconsin	Circuit Court
Wyoming	District Court
Wash., D.C.	Superior Court (Probate Division)

APPENDIX B
States Recognizing Nuncupative Wills

Personal Property only Limited by:

Indiana (1000)
Kansas (none)
Missouri (500)
New Hampshire (100)
 (No limit if made in presence of 3 witnesses)
Ohio (none)
Tennessee (1000)
 ($10,000 for military in time of war)
Texas (30)
 (No limit if made in presence of 3 witnesses)
Vermont (200)
Washington (1000)
 (No limit if in military or mariners)

Real and Personal Property Limited by:

Mississippi (100)
 (No limit if made in presence of 2 witnesses)
Nevada (1000)
South Carolina
 (No limit if made in presence of 3 witnesses)
Louisiana
 (Must be witnessed, reduced in writing, signed by the testator
and the witnesses)

Real and Personal Property No Limit

Georgia
North Carolina

Only by Persons in the Military and Mariners

Alaska
Massachusetts
New York
Oklahoma (1000)
Rhode Island
 (Valid for personal property only)

South Dakota (1000)
Virginia
West Virginia
Wash., D.C.
 (Valid for personal property only)

Nuncupative Will Not Recognized

Alabama
Arizona
Arkansas
California
Colorado
Connecticut
Delaware
Florida
Hawaii
Idaho
Illinois
Iowa
Kentucky
Maine
Maryland
Michigan
Minnesota
Montana
Nebraska
New Jersey
North Dakota
Oregon
Pennsylvania
Utah
Wisconsin
Wyoming

APPENDIX C
States Recognizing Holographic Wills

In Testator's Handwriting Signed by Testator

Alaska

Arizona

Arkansas
  (3 witnesses must establish that entire body of the will and signature are in testator's handwriting)

California
  (Date required under certain conditions)

Idaho

Kentucky

Maine

Mississippi

Montana

Nebraska
  (Date required under certain conditions)

New Jersey

North Carolina
  (3 witnesses must establish that entire body of the will and signature are in testator's handwriting. 1 witness must testify that the document was found among testator's valuable papers)

North Dakota

Pennsylvania

Tennessee
  (2 witnesses must establish this)

Texas
  (2 witnesses must establish this, or testator can execute and attach a self-proving affidavit)

Utah

Virginia
  (2 witnesses must establish this)

West Virginia

Wyoming

In Testator's Handwriting Signed by Testator Dated
Louisiana
  (2 witnesses must establish this)
Michigan
Nevada
Oklahoma
South Dakota

Only by Persons in the Military and Mariners
Maryland
New York

Holographic Wills Not Recognized
Alabama
Connecticut
Delaware
Florida
Georgia
Hawaii
Illinois
Indiana
Iowa
Kansas
Massachusetts
Minnesota
Missouri
New Hampshire
New Mexico
Ohio
Oregon
Rhode Island
South Carolina
Vermont
Washington
Wisconsin
Washington, D.C.

APPENDIX D
Uniform Probate Code Adopting States

Code Adopted

Alaska
Arizona
Colorado
Idaho
Maine
Montana
Nebraska
New Mexico
North Dakota
Utah

One or More Articles or Parts Adopted

Arkansas
Georgia

APPENDIX E

Spouse Omitted from Will Because of Will Executed After Marriage

UPC

Alabama
Alaska
Arizona
Colorado
Florida (other exceptions)
Hawaii
Idaho
Maine
Michigan
Minnesota
Missouri
Montana
Nebraska
New Jersey
New Mexico
Nevada (other exceptions)
North Dakota
Oregon
Pennsylvania
Utah
Washington (other exceptions)
Wisconsin

Marriage Does Not Revoke Will

Arkansas
Delaware
Illinois
Indiana
Iowa
Kansas (marriage and birth of child does)
Louisiana
Maryland (marriage and birth of child does)
Mississippi
New Hampshire (marriage and birth of child does)
New York
North Carolina

Ohio
Oklahoma (marriage and birth of child does; unless will shows
 intention to omit)
Tennessee (marriage and birth of child does)
Texas
Virginia
Wyoming
Washington, D.C. (marriage and birth of child does)

Will Revoked As To Spouse
California (unless will shows intention to omit; has other
 exceptions)

Will Revoked
Connecticut (marriage revokes will unless contingency provided
 for)
Georgia (marriage revokes will unless will comtemplates the
 marriage)
Kentucky (marriage revokes will unless shows contrary intent;
 marriage revokes will unless contingency provided for)
Massachusetts (marriage revokes will unless will contemplates
 the marriage)
Rhode Island (marriage revokes will unless will contemplates
 the marriage)
South Carolina (marriage revokes will unless spouse provided
 for by the will)
South Dakota (has other exceptions)
West Virginia (marriage revokes will unless contingency provided for)

Law Not Covered
Vermont

APPENDIX F
Omission of Child Will When Born After Execution of Will

UPC
Alabama
Arizona
Alaska
Colorado
Florida
Hawaii
Idaho
Indiana
Kentucky
Maine
Missouri
Montana
Nebraska
New Jersey
New Mexico
North Dakota
Utah
Wisconsin

Will Not Revoked When Future Child Corn
Kansas (but marriage after will executed and child born revokes will)

Void As To Child
Arkansas (if child is neither named nor provided for in will)
California (unless omission intentional or provided for outside will)
Delaware (unless will dictates otherwise)
Illinois (not void if will shows omission intentional)
Iowa (unless omission intentional or provided for outside will)
Maryland (if not intentionally omitted, child

Massachusetts (unless omission intentional or provided for outside will)
Michigan (unless will provides for child)
Minnesota (unless omission intentional or provided for outside will)

133

Nevada (unless omission intentional or provided for outside will)

New Hampshire (unless will provides for child)

North Carolina (unless will provides for child or shows intention to omit)

Ohio (child cannot, however, receive property left to surviving spouse; unless will provides for child or shows intention to omit)

Oklahoma (unless omission intentional or provided for outside will)

Pennsylvania (child, however, cannot receive property left to surviving spouse; not void if will shows omission intentional)

Rhode Island (unless will provides for child or shows intention to omit)

South Carolina (but if there were other children before will executed, their shares reduced to give omitted child equal share)

Tennessee (unless omission intentional or provided for outside will)

Vermont (unless will provides for child or shows intention to omit)

Washington (if child is neither names not provided for by will)

West Virginia (if child is neither named nor provided for by will)

Will Revoked

Connecticut (future born child revokes will unless contingency provided for)

Georgia (future born child revokes will unless will contemplates future born child)

Louisiana (many exceptions)

APPENDIX G
Will Revoked by Divorce or Annulment After Execution of Will

UPC

Alaska (rights revived by re-marriage to former spouse)
Alabama (rights revived by re-marriage to former spouse)
Arizona (rights revived by re-marriage to former spouse)
Arkansas
Colorado (rights revived by re-marriage to former spouse)
Delaware (rights revived by re-marriage to former spouse)
Florida (annulment does not revoke provision for spouse)
Hawaii
Idaho (rights revived by re-marriage to former spouse)
Illinois
Indiana
Iowa (rights revived by re-marriage to former spouse)
Kansas (plus property settlement revokes provision for former spouse)
Maine (rights revived by re-marriage to former spouse)
Michigan (rights revived by re-marriage to former spouse; unless will provides otherwise)
Minnesota (rights revived by re-marriage to former spouse)
Missouri (annulment does not revoke provision for spouse)
Montana (rights revived by re-marriage to former spouse)
Nebraska (rights revived by re-marriage to former spouse)
New Jersey (unless will provides otherwise)
New Mexico (rights revived by re-marriage to former spouse)
North Carolina (annulment does not revoke provision for spouse)
North Dakota (rights revived by re-marriage to former spouse)
Ohio (rights revived by re-marriage to former spouse)
Oklahoma (rights revived by re-marriage to former spouse)
Pennsylvania (annulment does not revoke provision for former spouse)
South Carolina (annulment does not revoke provision for spouse)
Tennessee (plus property settlement revokes provision for former spouse)
Texas (rights revived by remarriage to former spouse)

135

Utah (right revived by re-marriage to former spouse)
Virginia (annulment does not revoke provision for spouse)
Washington (annulment does not revoke provision for spouse)
Wisconsin

GLOSSARY OF LEGAL TERMS

Abatement: A reduction of a legacy under a will which occurs when the assets in the estate are insufficient to pay all cash legacies (*i.e.*, there are not enough assets to pay bequests in full).

Ademption: The elimination of a bequest in a will, because the asset bequeathed is no longer in existence at the time of death. Such a bequest is said to be "adeemed."

Administration: The process of managing a descendant's estate. Sometimes referred to as a "probate administration" or "probate."

Administration expenses: Those expenses incurred in connection with probating an estate.

Administrator: In the event a person dies without a will or the will fails to name the representative, the representative will be appointed by the probate court.

Administratix: A female administrator.

Advancement: A lifetime payment intended to be "on account of" a beneficiary's bequest under a will or an heir's intestate share. If the payment is an advancement, it will be deducted from the beneficiary's inheritance.

Age of majority: This is the time when a person is legally able to manage his/her own affairs and no longer considered a minor.

Ancillary administration: Sometimes it is necessary to have probate proceedings conducted in more than one state. Typically, there will be a probate commenced in the state where the individual resided (called the domicilary administration) and in any other state where the individual owned real property (called an ancillary administration).

Annual exclusion: This is the $3000 which, under the Internal Revenue Code may be given to each donee tax-free each year ($6000 if the gift is of community property or separate property, where the donor's spouse joins in the gift). Such gifts are "excluded" in applying gift tax rules.

Annuity trust: A trust providing for the payment of a specified amount monthly, yearly, or at some other interval, as distinguished from a trust providing for payments measured

137

by a percentage of the value of the trust (a unitrust) or providing for payment of the income generated by the trust assets.

Bequest: A legacy is sometimes called a bequest and usually refers to the giving of money.

Caveat: A person objecting to the will files an objection which is called a *caveat*.

Caveator: A person filing a caveat is a caveator or a contestant. Caveatrix is a female caveator.

Codicil: An amendment to a will. The requirements for execution of a codicil are the same as those for a will.

Co-executors: It is possible to have more than one person as an executor, and in such case the executors are called co-executors.

Common law: The law developed in England through the decisions of judges. The term "common law" is sometimes used to distinguish case law from statutory law (*i.e.*, laws adopted by a legislative body).

Community property: In the eight states using the community property system (Arizona, California, Idaho, Louisiana, Nevada, New Mexico, Texas, and Washington) this is property acquired by a married person through his or her efforts, skill, or labor during marriage and while domiciled in a community property state.

Conservator: A person, bank, or trust company appointed to manage the assets of an adult not legally capable of managing his/her own financial affairs (called a "conservator of the estate") or appointed to be responsible for the physical custody and care of an adult unable properly to care for himself/herself (called a "conservator of the person"). In many states the functions and duties of guardians and conservators are similar; in others there are no guardians for adults, only conservators. The person for whom the conservator is responsible is called a "conservatee."

Corpus: principle: The assets (property) in a trust are called the corpus or the principal.

Curtesy: Under the old English law, this was the interest in a deceased wife's property to which her husband was entitled regardless of the provisions of the wife's will. In most non-community property states this has been replaced by forced heirship rights or a right of election.

Devise: The disposition of realty by will. In strict legal terminology, a gift of real estate in a will is a devise, a gift of cash in a will is a legacy, and a gift of other personal property (such as stock or tangible property) is a bequest. In modern legal terminology the tendency is to use the term *bequest* for all three kinds of testamentary gifts. The person to whom the devisor leaves property is called the *devisee.*

Dower: A widow's right, under the old English law, to the income from a portion of her husband's assets. In most non-community property states this has been replaced by "forced heirship" statutes or statutes giving the surviving spouse a "right of election" to take a certain percentage of the deceased spouse's assets regardless of testamentary disposition. The husband's counterpart of dower is "curtesy." The community property system does not provide for dower or curtesy.

Escheat: A reversion of property to the state government for want of any individual in line to inherit the property. Assets escheat if the deceased person does not leave a will and has no living heirs.

Executor: An individual or institution (such as a bank or trust company) designated in a will to be responsible for the administration of the estate of the person making the will.

Fee simple: Developed in English property law, this term means unrestricted outright ownership or real property, as distinguished from a lease, ownership for a limited period of time, or one of the restricted forms of ownership which existed under the old English law.

Fiduciary: Any individual who owes a responsibility to another. In the estate planning field, it is a generic term covering executors, administrators, trustees, conservators, guardians, and other individuals or institutions with the responsibility of managing the property for the benefit of others.

Forced heirship right: The right of a spouse or other relative to take a portion of a deceased person's estate even against the wishes of the deceased person. Such a right is typically implemented by granting the holder a "right of election" to take a share of the estate notwithstanding the provisions of the will.

Foreign will: A will of a deceased person who resided in another state.

139

Grantor: The person who establishes a trust. In some states this person is called a "trustor" or a "settlor." The three terms are synonymous.

Guardian ad litem: A person appointed by the court to represent and protect an infant in a legal proceeding. This guardian is temporary and has no power over the infant's person or property.

Heir: If a person dies without a will his or her heirs will inherit the property. An individual's heirs are the persons who would inherit the property if he or she were to die intestate.

Intestate: Having died without a will.

Issue: Children, grandchildren, and others directly descending from a common ancestor. If a distribution under a will or trust is made "to issue," ordinarily descendants of a deceased child receive the share which the child would have taken, and descendants of a living child (though they are technically issue) do not inherit.

Joint tenancy: A method of co-ownership between two or more persons under which the interest of a deceased co-owner passes automatically to the surviving owner or owners unaffected by the will of the deceased co-owner. This "right of survivorship" distinguishes joint tenancy from *tenancy in common*.

Legacy: If a person leaves personal property to someone by will he or she has made a legacy.

Legatee: Someone who receives a cash bequest (a legacy) under a will. The term is often used to refer to anyone who inherits under a will.

Letter of administration: The document issued by a court to the administrator of an estate evidencing his, her, or its appointment.

Letters testamentary: Document issued by the court to an executor (or executrix) of an estate evidencing his/her or its appointment.

Liquidity: This is the cash (or property readily convertible into cash) in an estate which can be used to pay the debts of the estate and the expenses of administration.

Living trust: A trust created during a person's lifetime.

Marital deduction-estate tax: A deduction established under the Internal Revenue Code which is, generally speaking, equal to the greater of (a) one-half of the net separate property passing from the descendant to his/her surviving spouse or (b) the sum of $250,000, less one-half of any community property owned by the descendant and his spouse. Complex rules govern what constitutes property passing to a surviving spouse and how the precise amount of the deduction is calculated.

Per capita: A form of distribution under a will or trust which is an alternative to a per stirpes (*see, Per stirpes* below) distribution. Under a per capita distribution, grandchildren or more remote descendants on the same level share fractions of the estate which their parents would have taken.

Personal representative: A person legally empowered to clean up the unfinished business of a deceased person.

Per stirpes: A Latin phrase frequently used in wills which means "by the root." It is the method of distribution under a will or trust by which descendants step into the shoes of an ancestor. Thus, if a testator provided for per stirpes distribution and had a deceased son survived by one child and a deceased daughter survived by three children, the son's child would receive one-half of the estate and the daughter's children would receive one-sixth. Thus, the three children of the daughter divide the share which would otherwise have gone to their mother. (This is to be distinguished from a per capita distribution, under which the four grandchildren would share equally, so that the son's child would receive one-fourth of the estate). Another translation of per stirpes is "principle of representation."

Pour-over will: A will directing that assets (typically the residue of the estate) shall be added to a trust either established by the testator during lifetime, or established by another individual during lifetime, or occasionally established by the will of another individual.

Power of appointment: The power to direct the disposition of property held in trust.

Power of attorney: A document authorizing one individual (the attorney-in-fact) to act as agent on behalf of another individual (the principal). The attorney-in-fact can buy and sell assets on the principal's behalf and create other contractual obligations which are binding on the principal.

Probate: The process of administering a deceased person's estate. A will is said to be "admitted to probate" when a court decrees that it is genuine and executed in accordance with the formalities required by the law governing the court.

Probate court: The propounder files the application to probate the will in the court that handles such matters. Most states call this court the Probate Court (*see* Appendix A).

Propounder: The person who seeks to prove the will in court. Usually, but not always, the propounder is the person named in the will of the executor.

Remainderman: The person entitled to receive the assets in a trust upon the trust's termination.

Residuary clause or **Residuary bequest:** The portion of a will disposing of the residue of the estate (*i.e.*, the assets remaining after specific bequests have been satisfied and all taxes and expenses of administration have been paid).

Residuary estate: The assets remaining in the estate after all taxes, administration expenses, and specific bequests have been satisfied.

Reversionary trust: An arrangement whereby one or more beneficiaries receive benefits from a trust for a particular period of time after which the trust assets revert to the person who originally established the trust (called the *grantor, settlor,* or *trustor*). The interest of the grantor in the trust is called the "reversion" or reversionary interest, and the process of the assets returning to the grantor is called *reversion.* If the assets ultimately pass to someone other than the grantor, that interest is called a "remainder."

Revocable trust: An arrangement whereby the person setting up the trust retains the power to require that the trust terminate and the assets return to him/her.

Right of election: The right given by statute (typically to a surviving spouse) to take a portion of the deceased person's estate notwithstanding the provisions of the descendant's will (sometimes called forced heirship right).

Rule against perpetuities: The common law rule which limits the duration of trusts (other than those established for charitable purposes). Most wills and trusts contain a "perpetuities savings clause" designed to prevent the plan of distribution in the will or trust from violating the rule against perpetuities.

Rules of inheritance: Every state has rules stating who are a deceased person's heirs. These heirs are defined by the Rules

142

of Inheritance. The Rules of Inheritance are sometimes referred to as the Statutes of Descent and Distribution and sometimes as the Statutes of Intestate Succession.

Settlor: The person who establishes a trust. In some jurisdictions known as a "grantor" or a "trustor." These terms are synonymous.

Short-term trust: The terms "short-term" trust, "Clifford" trust, and sometimes "ten-year" trust are used interchangeably. They all refer to the tax-oriented arangements whereby assets are placed in trust either for a specified period of time (not less than ten years) or for the lifetime of the trust beneficiary and revert to the person who established the trust.

Spendthrift trust: A trust in which the interest of the beneficiary cannot be attached or otherwise collected by his or her creditors and also may not be sold, given away, or otherwise transferred by the beneficiary. The effectiveness of spendthrift clauses has been limited by statute and by case law in the various jurisdictions.

Tangible personal property: Property which may be possessed physically, such as furniture, furnishings, jewelry, and automobiles, as distinguished from intangible personal property such as stock, savings accounts, and bonds.

Tenants by the entirety: A special kind of joint tenancy which can exist only between husbands and wives. Its principal effect is that the assets held in this fashion pass automatically to the surviving spouse on the death of either spouse.

Tenancy in common: A method of co-ownership between two or more persons under which the interest of a deceased co-owner passes in accordance with his/her will, or, if there is no will, in accordance with the laws of intestate succession.

Testamentary guardian: A person named in the will of the last surviving parent to be the new parent of the orphan child. Guardianship may be of the person, of the property, or of both.

Testamentary trust: A trust created by a will at the time of death.

Testator or **Testatrix:** A person who makes a will. When a person dies, if that person has a will he/she dies testate. Thus a person dies either testate or intestate, with a will or without a will.

INDEX

INDEX

148